HOW THE
RATS
RE-FORMED
THE CONGRESS

HOW THE
RATS
RE-FORMED
THE CONGRESS

RALPH NADER

CSRL
Washington, DC

CSRL
P.O. Box 19367
Washington, DC 20036

Library of Congress Control Number: 2018952975
ISBN: 978-0-936758-08-4 (hardcover)
ISBN: 978-0-936758-13-8 (paperback)

Printed in the USA.

First Edition 2018

9 8 7 6 5 4 3 2 1

To Russell who provided the empiricism.

To the spirit of Voltaire and Mark Twain.

*To Molly Ivins, Dick Gregory, Jim Hightower, and Victor Navasky
who taught us how to laugh ourselves seriously.*

Invader

It was one of those uncomfortable morning strategy sessions with his senior staff. For House Speaker Reginald Blamer, the discomfort was in having to figure ways to continue blocking a long overdue raise in the federal minimum wage for many millions of low income workers when he knew in his gut that it was not the right thing to do. "We're in the crosshairs," he would say, starting such Congressional meetings in his spacious office. Not that his anxiety would cause him to renege on the implicit promise he made to the Big Boys to stop the move in Congress to raise the minimum. But there was still background anxiety. After all, politicians are only human, and, like many, Speaker Blamer came from a large family that had lived through tightened circumstances. His father was a tavern-keeper and his mother a seamstress. Deep anxiety, however, did have one inherent comfort at such morning gatherings; it tended to work in mysterious ways to overcome his morning constipation—the constant bane of the Speaker's existence. Holding down thirty million American workers—included among them many conservative voters, who, when adjusted for inflation, are making less today than workers made in 1968—bothered the very private, self-censored, psychosomatic recesses of the Speaker's conscience.

And so, not surprisingly, Speaker Blamer felt the onset of a solid bowel movement. He excused himself and repaired to his large private bathroom. As he sat down on the broad porcelain toilet, he felt that the expected discharge would be ample and prompt—no straining today. After quick breaks of wind, the Speaker heard a sound inside the toilet. But it wasn't from his bowels. Lifting himself up a bit, he looked down and saw the head of a mostly submerged black rat closely eyeing his bottom. "YEEEOW, YEEEEOW, YEEEOW," bellowed the Speaker as he straightened up and slammed the cover down. Alarmed, the staff rushed to the bathroom door to respectfully call, "Speaker Blamer, are you all right? Do you need help?" They dared not open the door. The Speaker did not tolerate any exposure of his privacy, especially being seen in his corpulent native suit.

Another more normal person might have replied, "Yeah, I'm okay ... it's just that there was a rat in the toilet bowl." But Speaker Blamer was not a normal person. He has had to be super-cunning to get to his present station in life. Being cunning means you can instantly sense danger, being as alert as, say, a rat. And Speaker Blamer was already imagining the deriding head-lines and the late-night-show jokes if he disclosed what really prompted his impulsive cries of sheer terror as he leapt from the "throne." So he replied, "Nothing much boys, just one of those sudden spasms I get once in a while. Sure comes on fast and goes away fast too. I'll be right out."

Rejoining the staff at the head of the conference table, albeit full of gas and un-discharged wastes, the Speaker went through the checklist for crushing the hopes of the downtrodden multitudes. His chief of staff reviewed the usual elements of the campaign against workers. First off, the Speaker will say, "I always thought that if you raise the price of anything, you get less of it. The proposal to raise the minimum wage is a Job Killer!"

"Good sound bite," said his research assistant.

The Speaker nodded gravely, though when he heard the word "bite" he silently winced.

The operations assistant counted off the usual, reliable economics professors, who would supply "objective" warnings about losses of jobs and recession. The fast food and big box retailer association had begun the large ad-buy on television and radio with the announcers' stentorian voices of dire gravity. The K Street lobbyists were already in action on Capitol Hill, marshaling the corporate PACS to make sure this drive was on the front burner, hinting to legislators that their employers might see this as a litmus test for their donations. Op-eds, letters to the editors, and editorial condemnation of economically disruptive higher wages and layoffs were already in the pipeline.

About to burst, the Speaker could not wait to end the meeting. "OK, fel-lows, you seem to have the situation well in hand—it's not the first time we had to fight off this wage grab. Get to work." They all scattered, including an irreverent intern who wondered to herself whether paying members of Congress more would mean the government would end up with less of *them*.

The moment the door to his spacious office closed, the Speaker literally lunged to his private toilet whereupon he unloaded a vast quantity of feces: soft and semi-hard. Three bursts worth. Before he could enjoy a moment of quiet satisfaction, a shrill shriek lifted him up as his eyes bulged. It was the black rat swimming in the bowl propelling the terrified cry—"YEEEOW, YEEEOW, YEEEOW!" Again he slammed down the toilet seat, kept his hand on the flush handle, gritting his teeth as if to say: "On the way to oblivion, you dirty rat!"

His longtime secretary heard his yell and rushed to his bathroom. "Mr. Speaker, Mr. Speaker, what happened? Are you OK?"

Recovering his composure, he replied, "I'm OK, Sarah, just more of those sudden spasms. I've got to get some physical therapy. By the way, did you schedule that fund-raiser next week for an hour later?"

"Yes, I did, Mr. Speaker," Sarah replied, sounding very relieved.

Arriving home that early evening, he sat down to a healthy diet supper prepared by his adoring wife Regina. Their three children were grown up, living in distant states, so they were "empty nesters."

"You seem unusually agitated, honey," said Regina. "Did you have a hard day?"

"It seems every day is a hard day in these times," he replied, shrugging off her concern. "What a great meal always, Regina! Now I need some relaxing reading. Do you know where we put that colorful book of animals that we got as a wedding anniversary gift years ago?"

"Why yes, Reginald. It came in three volumes: mammals, reptiles, and insects. Tell me which one you want and I will get it for you."

"Mammals," he replied.

Sitting in his study the Speaker started reading about the rat. The word "rat" is derived from the Latin "*rodere*" which means "to gnaw." Rats produce litters several times a year, with high infant mortality. If seen as weak, newborns are eaten by their parents and their stronger siblings. Over the centuries, rats have developed uncanny abilities to survive dangers everywhere, especially those produced by their close proximity to humans, whose detritus and garbage ironically provide the means by which they prosper and create new nests. Rats live everywhere: underground, in sewers, in buildings, highways, yards, cellars. They also wander to get food, which may involve killing any mammals smaller than they, including mice. They also eat insects. Their appetite is immense, facilitated by their sharp teeth. This leads some intrepid rats to wander into little known crevices and, yes, pipes. Restaurant kitchens and their refuse attract them since these animals have a strong sense of smell. Then the Speaker saw the words, "They even like feces."

The Speaker had enough. But before he closed the book, he saw a footnote citing some conversations that bloggers had with frightened people asking about rats swimming up the toilet bowl. The Speaker went to the sites. He learned that when sewer lines are in disrepair or when storms overpower the sewer system, sewer rats see an opportunity. Sure, most everybody knows that rats can run, climb, and leap up to three feet. Fewer know that rats can gnaw through concrete. Even fewer know what an impossibly tiny space rats can squeeze themselves through when they smell food or prey. And who knows that rats can tread water for three days and can swim over a half mile to reach dry ground?

Flushing is a very temporary fix, for a rat can hold its breath until the water passes. Rats can even come down from the roof by going through the soil pipeline, then through the vent and down the pipe into the toilet. "Rats can always find a way if there is one," one plumber was quoted as saying. The Speaker scrolled down to a section titled, "Rats and Bubonic Plague, Typhus, and Rabies..." This time he really had enough and switched off his computer, retiring to his chambers somewhat nauseous.

Repeat Performance

The next morning at the office, he felt the urge and went into his bathroom, flushed the toilet three times, and sat down to do his business. It took about four minutes for the bowel movements to seriously commence, thanks to the unsung sphincter, when he felt something like a brush across his testicles. Springing up and looking down, he saw the black rat waving its whiskered head back and forth. "EEEEYOW, EEEYOW," the Speaker shrieked at the top of his lungs. Once again his secretary rushed to the door to see if he was in need of help.

Ralph Nader

"It's that awful spasm again, Sarah. I'd better see the house doctor. Can you get me an appointment early tomorrow morning?" (He felt awful lying, but there was no choice.) The rat was still splashing around languidly, as if it were taking a bath, by the time he slammed down the toilet cover. He kept flushing the toilet until his back hurt. Quickly he got a bottle of alcohol from the cabinet and poured it into his hand with which he cuddled his balls to disinfect what he could. For good measure, he poured hydrogen peroxide into a cupped hand and rested his balls in that antiseptic liquid.

It turned out that as Sarah returned to her desk, she found the Reporter waiting for one of the Speaker's assistants who had agreed to be interviewed about some appropriations earmarked for the Speaker's district. He, too, heard the "EEEYOW, EEEYOW."

"Who's that?" he asked, knowing it came from the Speaker's suite.

"Sometimes the water comes out scalding hot and it catches the person under the shower unaware," Sarah answered. (She felt awful lying, but there was no choice.)

Meanwhile, the Speaker, about to burst, had to find an outlet to receive his deposits. Terror-stricken, he sat down on the edge of the bathtub and let it all out, come what may. Fortunately, the stools were very loose and he quickly washed them down the drain with a tumbler filled with water. He then showered, dried himself, and dressed.

He was late for a meeting over the bill to weaken the Endangered Species Act. The get-together was with the Chairman of the Committee, a guy who hated wolves, a prejudice he had picked up from his upbringing on a cattle ranch in Montana. The Chairman, whom the Speaker found surrounded by four grim-looking staffers, was determined to gut the law. The Speaker asked the Chairman whether he would add an amendment to make rats and cockroaches *more endangered* as species. Everyone thought the Speaker was being funny and didn't reply. The Speaker did not persist, going along with the chuckles to mask his inner turmoil.

More Bathroom Business

Over at the Minority Leader's suite, the dignified Marcy Melosay was finishing some camouflaged fund-raising calls (ones absent a direct ask) when she felt nature's call. She, too, had trouble moving bowels early in the morning. She always admired colleagues who could immediately defecate upon rising from bed. Never in her twenty-eight years in the House could she acquire that blessing, that relief from feeling bloated and gassy. As a female public official, she had to be especially careful about farting even when the gasses were building up to the breaking point. At extreme moments she would excuse herself by appearing to have a coughing jag, go to her spacious bathroom, and sonorously break wind. "Ahh, thank goodness, I made it in time," she would say to herself.

Today, it was almost noon when she excused herself, but not before telling her assistant to call her sister-in-law and cancel tomorrow's breakfast. The Minority Leader made a beeline to her own toilet, plunked herself down, and commenced serious discharge. She heard a noise. Lifting herself up, she saw a black rat smothered with fresh feces. The reaction from her was an ear-splitting, prolonged scream, "AHHHH-HHHH, AHHHHH, AHHHHKHEEE." Startled, the rat scurried back down the pipe as the Minority Leader ran from the throne, soiling the floor and nearly tripping on her panties, up to the sink where she rested her trembling hands. Her long-time assistant, Velvet, rushed to the bathroom door exclaiming, "Miss Melosay, Miss Melosay, do you need anything?"

"Yes, please," the Minority Leader responded just above a whisper. Velvet rushed in and her beloved boss told her what happened between gasps of breath.

A matronly sixty-six year old, Velvet cradled Ms. Melosay in her arms and assured her that all is well when it ends well. The rat was probably scared, too, she added reassuringly. The Minority Leader managed a wan smile, though she continued to shake uncontrollably. "You may wish to have a bath to calm yourself down and soothe your nerves, Ms. Melosay," Velvet suggested. The diminutive Minority Leader nodded and let Velvet turn on the bathwater so she could have a very long soak. Again, the Reporter just happened to be in the sitting room and heard the screams.

Synchronicity

The next noon, the Speaker and the Minority Leader found themselves together at a Joint Session of Congress to honor the return of American Israeli soldiers from crushing defenseless Gaza again with weapons made in America. The keynote speaker was the Prime Minister of Israel, whose past presentations before this august body had rated standing applause coming (on the average) after every thirty-five words. Going through both their minds at the same time was the fear that standing ovations of such frequency would trigger an uncontrollable surge of defecation. Excusing themselves in the midst of this command performance would be disastrous, for without admitting the cause, which would have provoked muffled guffaws, the Speaker and the Minority Leader might be unfairly accused of thinly veiled anti-Semitism. Talk about being between a rock and a hard place.

The standing ovations continued with staccato predictability and reached a crescendo when the Prime Minister declaimed loudly that he was amazed that people didn't realize Iran was the biggest threat to the world since Hitler. It was also amazing, if of less global significance, that when under enormous pressure to contain one's bodily emissions, there is an impressive display of the discipline known as mind over matter. Immediately after the thirty-second and last standing ovation, the Speaker quickly and profusely thanked the Prime Minister and the soldiers and adjourned the session. Both he and the Minority Leader literally raced to their respective restrooms for immediate relief. The same canny Reporter noticed their respective beelines and began to wonder.

For a couple of days whenever nature called, the Speaker and the Minority Leader made some excuse to use the staff's toilet because they couldn't stand the return of the cold fear they'd experienced in their boudoirs. Lo and behold, one day the staff's toilets were occupied, so they both nervously sat down in their respective spaces and, once again, in the midst of doing their business, they heard, they raised, they looked, and they screeeeeched at the top of their lungs. There was a black, grinning rat in each bowl.

They did what they had to do. The Speaker drained his bathtub. The Minority Leader had to finish her business in her shower stall since, being in the minority, she was not allotted a bathtub. The confidential Velvet learned what had happened to her leader while the Speaker's staff heard about the spasm again. Having not gotten his interview earlier, the same Reporter returned and heard the screams again coming from the Minority Leader's interior office suite. His wonder turned into operational curiosity.

The Minority Leader warned Velvet to tell no one about what happened. "NO ONE!"

"Why, of course," Velvet replied in a tone that suggested such an admonition was not needed. Leader Melosay told Velvet to get the Speaker on the phone immediately.

A Call to Action

The Speaker picked up his phone to take the call from the Minority Leader. "Speaker," she told him calmly, "we have a rodent problem. They've been seen scurrying around the carpets in recent days, both rats and mice, which means there are nests. They are probably coming up from the catacombs beneath the Capitol." (The Minority Leader hated to lie but there was no choice.) She asked the Speaker to request an inspection by the rodent and insect extermination unit, which was under the House Administration Committee's jurisdiction.

Of course, the Speaker assured her he would do so immediately and revealed that he too had been told by staff that the little creatures were running all over their carpets too. (He hated to lie but there was no choice). The Minority Leader asserted that this rodent invasion must be systemic and she joked about a rare bipartisan display of pending remedial action. Lowering his voice, the Speaker suggested that the requested action should be seen as a very routine inspection to avoid the press making more of it than was deserved. The Minority Leader, possessed of similarly sensitive political antennae, agreed, and before closing requested that her office be given advance notice of the inspectors' arrival and told what kinds of rodenticide they employ.

"Will do," said the Speaker. "Talk to you soon."

However, for the Speaker, the matter was not so simple. Suppose the inspectors find nothing, not a hole, not a hair, not a dropping, but not wanting to disappoint their superiors, they recommend some rat poison be placed around the suites. The Speaker knew that would not solve his problem, which was the toilet! He could not, would not, give away his secret to the inspectors that rats were bobbing around in his personal commode for then there would be an inevitable leak. Between the rat in the toilet and the yelling, people would start putting two and two together. With over four hundred and fifty fulltime, snooping reporters covering Capitol Hill—"ditto heads," he derisively calls them—plenty would rush to pursue this story. "They always have an anal complex," the Speaker thought to himself, chuckling over his own wit.

He decided to let his exterminators do what they urged if only because their application provided a cover for any later media inquiry. Within a few hours, poison bait and rat traps were situated in circumspect locations around his suite. The Speaker called and told the Minority Leader to schedule a similar remedy for her offices.

Both the Speaker and the Minority Leader knew that this was not going to solve their own very personal problems. The individual rats were entering the toilet bowl from a pipe that was far removed from the rat traps. Each politician could not think of a way to tell the other what they were going through since they did not know they shared a common, horrifying experience. Such was their conundrum.

In the Underground

Meanwhile, down deep in the Capitol's underworld, activity of another sort was taking place. It was going on in a vast subterranean area where gigantic steam pipes sweat side by side with other engineering systems that keep the vast buildings above operating technically, if not legislatively. This is terrain so occupationally hazardous that no member of Congress, regardless of position or seniority, is allowed to enter the elevators and descend deeply to the bottom. The heavy metal particulates, including asbestos, and emissions, have long plagued the small number of security-cleared, skilled workers who complain, to no avail, about their chronic health problems.

For rodents and insects, however, the immense space was a favorite scampering (and camping) ground, but one with few ascending apertures. Except, that is, for the odorous sewage pipes. Rats and mice were curious about these laden pipes, but the water that washed them down was irritable to their fur. Far more tempting and preoccupying were the crumbs and foodstuffs left overnight or discarded by the workers.

Very recently, however, a startling development opened new opportunities for the rodents in their non-stop quest for nutrients. (Rats, as noted, were known to gnaw through concrete if they thought it would lead them to something tasty.) Both the Speaker and the Minority Leader, importuned by salespeople, had agreed to install electric garbage disposals in their kitchenette sinks. This was for the politicians' convenience when they did not have time to go to lunch or dinner and didn't particularly relish take-outs. Their staff could cook something up reflecting their bosses' tastes at the moment. Also, exercising a little *noblesse oblige*, our solons let the cleaning people use the cooking facility in the evening if these workers had to heat their take-outs. The cleaners were sternly instructed to leave no crumbs behind. But they let fall down through the grinders a stream of what the rats would call a dream banquet of flavorsome smoothies whose irresistible odor drew these hardy survivalists into bolder and bolder adventures in upward mobility. Soon the rats realized it was only a frolic and a detour to enter the sewer pipe to the toilet bowl. This would have been an easy connection to make by the exterminators if only they had been told the real story, which was that the rats were treating the toilet as a private oasis.

Rumblings

"What to do? What to do?" whispered the Speaker to himself, as he was busy over stacks of paperwork or conducting short meetings with legislative assistants and colleagues.

Before leaving for home, he called Regina and asked if he could have a big bowl of boiled prunes with a little ice cream for dessert. His wife understood and replied, "Why, of course, dear." Later at the dinner table, the Speaker consumed every last prune, washing them down with warm water to achieve the desired combination for an early morning bowel movement to be consummated in his home john. Alas, it was not to be. He left home still filled. However, by the time his limousine reached the House Office Building, he was feeling a rumble—the deferred prune effect—that reached an intolerable level, nearly overcoming his suppressive mind control. He raced past a startled Sarah into his restroom and, taking no chances, unloaded directly into his bathtub. "How long can this go on?" he asked himself while breathing a sigh of sublime relief.

Meanwhile, a few miles away at NSA Headquarters, a three-person surveillance team, specializing on Congress, was connecting certain strange dots. Their sensors had picked up the bellow, screams and conversations, including mutterings, of the Speaker and the Minority Leader. At first they suspected the rats were the products of animal-directed sabotage by terrorists. After all, the CIA, going back decades, had been expertly training ravens, dolphins, cats and other animals to be carriers for espionage activities. After spending several days, sifting and arranging the metadata, the team concluded that the precipitating events were just what they were: *ferae naturae* doing their instinctual thing. Not of concern. However, they parked the information in a specially encrypted electronic file titled, "To be *seeded* if necessary."

Two days later, the Reporter was sitting in the Minority Leader's office, having been given a rain check by staffer Joanna Swift, who had to cancel the prior appointment. Ms. Swift gave as her reason an emergency call that came in from a group of constituents in her boss's district. But the real cause of cancellation was that Ms. Swift was not fully prepared for the questions that this legendary, lone wolf Reporter could be expected to ask. (She hated to lie but there was no choice.)

At 11 am sharp, Ms. Swift bounded from her small office to cheerfully greet the reporter and usher him to a chair by her desk. "Sorry about last time," she said.

"Forget it; things happen," replied the Reporter. He adjusted his tape recorder and launched immediately into a touchy subject. "Before I get into my investigation of what your leadership is doing about timed, insider stock trading, revealed recently, as you know, by a freelance author, to be widespread in the House, I'm curious about something else. In the anteroom, I saw two large boxes labeled portable toilets. Is there something seriously wrong with the plumbing?" The Reporter looked casual in a "by the way" manner.

Ms. Swift blushed, but, suspecting his uncharacteristic casualness, felt it was better to reveal some of the truth, blurted out, "There's been a rodent problem we're having attended to by the House exterminators."

"Oh," said the Reporter. "That's not so infrequent, but in the toilets?"

"Well . . . yes, it actually has been quite frightening," she responded.

This is where experience comes in. The savvy Reporter skipped the usual follow-up inquiry—"What do you mean?"—and probed, "So, that's what the screams were about from the Minority Leader's suite when I was here waiting the other day."

Ms. Swift felt a trap was about to be sprung. She wasn't supposed to know what only the Minority Leader and Velvet knew, but "mum's the word" has a notoriously short life in Congressional offices. Now she was facing double jeopardy: letting a reporter, no less, know what she wasn't supposed to know herself.

"I really don't know what you're talking about. Screams? I didn't hear any screams." She was on the side of the suite where the staffers did hear the screams. (She hated to lie but there was no choice.) "Can we get back to your interest in what the Minority Leader is doing about the report of insider trading among some of her fellow Democrats?"

"Yes, yes, by all means," rasped the Reporter, who knew he was on to what his colleagues would call a very high-rated story, but he decided it was best not to press any further with this inadvertent informer.

Out of the Bag

A couple of hours later, the Minority Leader returned to her offices and was pleased with the sight of the portable toilets. It wasn't fun exercising bowel movements in a shower stall. In a moment of collegiality, she called the Speaker and told him of her temporary solution. The Speaker, smiling to himself, told her that "great minds think alike," and that his portable toilets arrived today as well.

The Minority Leader wondered, "Does the plural mean that the problem has spread to other toilets in your suite?"

"Well, yes, as a matter of fact. How about for you?"

"It has. In another bathroom my assistant came upon a dead mouse floating in the bowl. She couldn't take it and had to go home early," averred the Minority Leader in an upset tone.

"Wow, wow, do you think the *rat* is out of the bag, so to speak?" said the Speaker with high concern.

"Not if I can help it, but I may not be able to help it," worried the Minority Leader.

"You took the words out of my mouth."

Ms. Melosay replied, "We'd better stay in close touch, Mr. Blamer."

Brought together by the common problem, they were already on a last name basis.

Party Time I

That night, the nocturnal rodents, down deep in the Congressional catacombs, were having a ball. More than bits of food were everywhere. Whole chunks had been cast aside by the workers who were celebrating the retirement of one of their crew; sadly, he had incurable emphysema. And what chunks: fish, chicken, and steak bones that were easily accessible in spilling-over, uncovered trash cans. The rats with their ever growing incisors loved the bones.

At the same time, the regular Thursday evening "small parties of relief," as they were called, were underway upstairs, put together by staffers whose bosses were returning to their districts until next week's Tuesday-through-Thursday period came around. The food digesters (i.e., garbage disposals) in the Speaker's and the Minority Leader's offices were kept busy, which in turn kept the sewer rats and mice deliciously busy, eating and populating. Well-fed and protected from most predators, the litters poured out of the mothers' wombs in their dark nests.

The staff, now using portables, flushed away quite a few visiting rats in the regular toilet bowls, now more with disgust than with fear. They still expected the exterminators to produce eventual eradication. The staff members were oblivious to the fact that the rat killers did not know about the toilet bowl visits and were concentrating their poisons and traps in nooks and crannies.

A Clean Breast

Arriving at home for dinner with Regina, the Speaker was unusually troubled as his wife recognized by noting how he raised his eyebrows in fast succession. His wife rarely saw such signs of deep worry. "Tell me, dear, what is eating at you these days? There is nothing in the news that could explain your vintage eyebrow flutters."

The Speaker sighed deeply, thinking that if he can't divulge what's been happening, his private personal secret, to his beloved wife of forty-two years, who knew every inch of his physical body, who else would he reveal it to? The moon? So he began.

"My dear, something is happening in my office. No, it doesn't involve great matters of state or whispers of some forthcoming exposé of corruption in the House of Representatives. To cut to the chase, it involves rats coming up my toilet while I am sitting … yes, sitting answering nature's call. I heard splashes and a rat brushed against my testicles before I leapt up with loud screams. When my staff came running, I made up the excuse that it was an old spasm acting up suddenly." He then recounted what transpired afterwards.

Regina was still puzzled. It wasn't her husband's fault in any way. "Why are you so upset," she asked?

The Speaker put down his fork and took a deep breath. "My dear, if this situation reached the media, it would be very serious for your poor husband. Politics is all about deception, distraction, and appearances. Take away the appearance, the decorum, the surface dignity and neatness, and all hell will start to break loose. Once we are mocked, satirized, and laughed at due to a story that is tailor-made for public ridicule by just about every part of the news and entertainment business, we will lose the sheen that glosses over what we're doing and not doing. That varnish is keeping us low in the polls, but not affecting our re-elections. It's about the consequences of the emperor having no clothes—literally!

"Consider the meticulous attention we give to appearances, to the protective gloss. We are immaculately dressed. You instinctually grasp this whenever, before I leave for work in the morning, you point out a slight slant to my tie or a wisp of hair sticking out of my coif. Notice that when you see members of Congress head for the floor with their entourage, you can always tell the legislator as the one who is erect, striding forward with confidence. Posture is crucial to an appearance of stature and dignity. It's maintained with aplomb by a legislator even after he's gone through such sordid exposes as that of being caught frequenting prostitutes, cheating on his wife, or thrashing others in alcoholic fits."

At this point, Regina wasn't sure if her husband was talking to her or giving a speech, but she listened patiently.

"Consider how daily attention by a large cleaning and maintenance staff is given to our offices, our corridors, our hearing rooms, the furniture, the flags, and the plaques. These are all symbols that protect our appearance of dignity. Take that dignity away and then the awe of power, affecting friend and foe, dissolves, and we descend to the level of despised next door neighbors. Why do you think our concise, level-toned statements to the press are so carefully scripted to prevent any slip of the tongue or eruption of raging emotions signifying lack of control?

"Bring up the subject matter of sexual parts being nearly nibbled (even fondled!) by rats, and the ranting of every two-bit radio/TV commentator, columnist, talk show host, cartoonist, plus every water-cooler conversation across the nation will go wild with ribald ridicule. And now there is the Internet—an endless vacuum for gossip already—and you've got the whole world guffawing and hungry for the latest development. And believe me, this is a story that will keep on giving, because as of now I don't see any light at the end of the tunnel if the episodes, which I suspect are also happening to Marcy Melosay, are not suppressed from public view."

"Marcy Melosay?" asked Regina with a wink of jealousy. "How do you know?"

"We've talked and I learned we've both ordered portable toilets, if you know what I mean . . ." the Speaker confided.

"How many people know the actual, intimate details?" she asked.

"I can't say. My entire office knows about the rats there, but how many know about the rats in the toilet with me sitting there depends on how many can connect my terrifying outcries from fear of the scurrying creatures on the floor to my fear of being emasculated on the throne.

"You know, Regina, if the exterminators continue to plant their rat poison and the rats keep coming, who is going to adhere to any oath or secrecy? It is just too good a conversation piece since everybody fears rodents and loves to talk about that fear; so it is not just a matter of protecting the boss. Sure, the story of rat infestation may be big enough to absorb my personal incident, but not if others are having the same experience when they are on their toilet. Going public will affect both the whole institution and each member, providing the greatest possible ammunition for taunting, jeering, mocking, and the asserting of utter Congressional incompetence.

Ralph Nader

"I can see the headlines: 'Rats Playing Catch with Lawmakers' Balls,' 'They Are Worth Something: Speaker's Balls Attract Rats,' 'Hungry Rats Invade House Toilet Bowls Spreading Terror Where the Sun Don't Shine,' 'Why is Speaker Blamer Screaming in His Bathroom?' 'Unlike the People, Rats Gain Access to Politicians.' And those, my dear, are just the first stage headlines, assuming the rat invasion goes no further."

By this time, Regina was convulsed with laughter. For the life of her, she couldn't take the matter as seriously as her husband did. "Don't worry, dear, the exterminators will take care of the rats. Meanwhile, why don't you wear that heavy jockstrap left over from your football playing days? It'll protect you from any first swipe and still leave your anus open for discharge. Just kidding. Have some more prunes to get you going early before you leave for work."

To the Next Level

In the next several days, two developments converged. The exterminators, who, in their professional zeal, wanted to leave no hiding place undisturbed, received permission to descend to the catacombs to place their rat poison everywhere. They saw lots of food-bits discarded by the workers. Their strategy was to get the rats before the rascals even thought of ascending through the pipes. The food thrown here and there will be the bait and the poison they added to the debris will finish the pests off.

As many humans have done in the past, they underestimated the intelligence of rats, who make connections, learn, and transfer their learning to their close kin. After some casualties, the rats figured the food placed near them was hazardous, and they started going back upstairs, accompanied by mice. They preferred the safety of the pipes going to the Speaker's and Minority Leader's splendid accommodations to the dangers of the tainted food. They were aided by another development. The nighttime workers had increased the discarded food sent down the digesters in order to keep down the volume of garbage they left behind, which might indicate the sizes of their supper and the time given over to its consumption.

One day, Speaker Blamer entered his bathroom to use his portable toilet only to see a mouse perched on the sink. The next day, he saw a young rat trapped in the bathtub. He bludgeoned the intruder to death with his large hair brush. "Ugh, ugh, ugh," he exclaimed. "I can't take this anymore." Whereupon he rushed into his office and dialed his special administrative assistant, Duke.

Duke, an ex-infantry captain, strode in smartly with an urgent message of his own to deliver. But first he had to hear out his boss.

"Duke, the exterminators cannot do the job by themselves. Get me the most aggressive cat you can find to stay here 24/7."

"Yes sir, on the double. But I have been instructed to tell you that the House Administrator has been receiving dozens of calls today. It seems that last night there was a mass invasion of rats and mice into the offices of scores of House members. It seems," he said, "that something happened below to drive them en masse from their lairs."

A preliminary inquiry revealed that the workers themselves had brought in several cats to drive away the rats whose keen scent detected the cats far and near. Thus, the flight northward occurred more quickly. The exterminators received a rush of calls from Republican and Democratic offices. Some staff went home in fright. The rat killers knew that the density of rats within the Congressional complex of buildings was much higher per person than elsewhere for two reasons. One was the absence of natural predators in so many secluded enclaves. Second was the presence of so many cafeterias, reception areas, vending machines, and exposed garbage disposals. Rat heaven!

Enter the Fourth Estate

The Reporter was putting the finishing touches on his core story about the rat incursions when he got a call from a tipster over at the House Administration Committee about the rat invasion. It looked like the whole thing was about to come to light. He called his editor to tell him that if he wanted a scoop he had "to move *prontissimo.*" The Reporter's crisp, wry, but factual narrative was sent in with the headline:

RATS AHOY! SPEAKER BLAMER AND MINORITY LEADER MELOSAY RECEIVE TERROR JOLT THAT NEARLY TOPPLES THEM FROM THEIR THRONES.

The editor wanted an even more racy title but the Reporter said no— it was his reputation at stake, not the editor's. He preferred a deadpan style, which he used as follows:

House Speaker Reginald Blamer and Minority Leader Marcy Melosay are like ordinary Americans in basic ways. About every day they have to defecate while at work. Recent days, however, have been a nightmare that few ordinary Americans have had to experience. Black rats have been surfacing in the toilet bowls of both legislators' private bathrooms at the exact moment when Mr. Blamer and Ms. Melosay were dropping their drawers to have a bowel movement. They had no advance warning so it was terrifying when they heard a rustling below them, only to look down to catch a horror in the making. Your reporter, by sheer coincidence, happened to be in both offices when the hair-raising screams were heard from the leaders' suites. Such outcries are not a usual auditory experience for visitors to the offices of Congressional legislators.

Reliable sources said that the purchase of portable toilets— which I saw delivered—was prompted by the invasion of rats apparently rising from the catacombs beneath Congress. Sources added that exterminators were called to position rat poison throughout the office suites. Yesterday's expansion of the rat invasion to other House of Representatives' offices is being attributed to the lack of garbage control and the retention of cats deep under the Congress by the underground workers, who were trying to contain or drive away the infestation of rodents. The rats fled the cats and found their way up the pipes to the lawmakers' bathrooms.

There is no evidence that the rats' incisors made any contact with the underbodies of Speaker Blamer and Minority Leader Melosay. No schedules were disrupted. The House Clinic was not visited on those days by the two solons.

With the spread of the rats to other offices, there are reports of terrified staff rushing home from their jobs out of stark fear. Rats are known to bring a variety of diseases and infection pathogens. As of this writing, the situation seems to be getting more dire and is nowhere near coming under control. The Congressional press corps is requesting a news briefing from both leaders inasmuch as rumors, some lurid, are outrunning the available facts. This is truly a breaking news story. There is much more information that the public has a right and need to know about. Check our website for up-to-the-minute postings.

The Reporter's story almost blew out the search engines. The visits, hits—call them what you will—came pouring down like a full blown avalanche in the Alps. The Reporter had told himself he wasn't going to lose a minute scrolling down to read comments on his story because this was a breaking story and he had to concentrate every moment on keeping ahead of his colleagues, who were now onto and joining the emerging bedlam.

Will it Never End?

Then what had to happen, happened! Loretta Langone, sitting at her computer working up material to be sent to the *Congressional Record* for her boss, Arkansas Congressman Sebastian Savant, felt something crawling up her ankle. She instinctively pulled back her foot and looked down to see a mouse with a death-grip on her sock. What happened next was the sound of "**AARGHASYEEEK**" as Ms. Langone fell backward, tipping her chair over as her knees upended her computer. The mouse dropped the sock, spun away, and disappeared from view. Her co-workers rushed over but Ms. Langone just lunged toward the door, ran down the wide corridors of the Russell House Office Building, down the stairwell, and out the door. She hailed a cab home, sobbing, breathing heavily, and shaking with fear as her imagination conjured up what further could have happened if the mouse had his way with her.

Of course, it was not long before a gaggle of reporters rushed to Congressman Savant's office only to find that their cell phones were ringing with news of other rodent-to-human-episodes in other Congressional offices. After a moment of cognitive dissonance, each went to what the newsperson believed to be the most newsworthy destination. To some that meant dashing to the Senate where all rat hell was breaking loose as the rodents were looking for pipes, apparently happy to be in ones not as crowded with fellow beasts as were those in the House plumbing. These reporters reasoned that senators are just bigger news.

Damage Control

Speaker Blamer began to experience the early stages of panic. He phoned Senate Majority Leader Horatio Clearwater to urge that they join together in closing the Congress for at least a day. Though he could visualize the expected headlines: "Rats Chase Politicians from Capitol Hill," he had to thwart further incidents and real panic. There could be blood on the floor. Senator Clearwater readily concurred but insisted that the Capitol Police stay on the job. "It wouldn't be good for morale and our law and order stance were they to be seen as being chased out by rats," he explained.

Since it was a Thursday, early in the Congressional session, there would be no appropriations or other legislative emergencies complicating the need for at least a three-day shutdown. The two also decided to call on President Winston DooLittle to proclaim a Congressional state of emergency—based on health and safety factors—in order to avail the Congress of the expert resources and assistance of the executive branch.

Speaker Blamer—the more politically savvy of the two—said they should immediately request the Centers for Disease Control dispatch teams that would highlight the diseases and pathogens that could emerge to spread beyond the confines of Congress. At his upcoming news conference, he would also note that rats were the carriers of the deadly bubonic disease, which as recently as the fourteenth century caused devastation in Europe. "Such menacing references," he asserted, "will direct the public's attention toward possible epidemics instead of allowing them to follow their natural inclination to treat the shutdown as a laugh fest."

Senator Clearwater responded with some skepticism as to whether this maneuver would work, but he concluded it was worth trying, especially if the Speaker had experts to back him up and could exhibit some killer rats at his press conference so that revulsion would replace the fast spreading derision. They both issued the order to evacuate all non-essential personnel until further notice.

Putting down the phone, the Speaker felt wet under his armpits—an unusual sign of stress. He closed his eyes, dreading the media's demand for an immediate press conference. Then he thought of a way to gain more time. He would tell the press (or rather his press officer would inform them) that he would go on Sunday's *Meet the Press* and answer any questions.

"He has to fully concentrate right now on defeating the rats," explained his press secretary to a crowd of raucous news-people.

The President quickly obliged the legislators by issuing an emergency proclamation, calling the rats "animal terrorists," which led him to further call up teams of special forces, the CIA, and the NSA to focus their talents on this city within a city called Congress and its 33,000 employees. "You can't negotiate with rats," he declared. "They have to be killed or captured."

Shutting down Congress had the benefit of shutting down the press—at least *in situ*. The reporters had to clear out of their Capitol Hill pressrooms along with the lawmakers and the staff. Even if the press people tried to find contacts on the Hill, they learned there was no one to talk to except the Capitol Police who were not talking. So they started working their cell phones and, when they got through occasionally to a possible source, soon found out that there weren't many new details except stories of fear, dread, and hot-footed escape. How many stories about such matters can you do? Moreover, Congressional staff was instructed to say very little to the media.

Ralph Nader

The Lay of the Media Land

The Reporter did his colorful stories to keep his website buzzing. But he knew the deeper news was the question of what was being done to the rats and, more importantly, what he saw as the looming political fallout from the masses. He got his answer to the first question when, moving down to the freight entrance, he saw trucks with cages of cats going into the garages. Following them, he saw the cat cages unloaded and taken by workers to various parts of the Capitol. The cats were not the languid pussycat types; they were mean alley cats and, as one unloader told him, "They are specially suited to pursue rats directly and to leave their urine around, which will scare off the rats they can't catch."

Once again the rats were underestimated. The urine scent simply drove them back into the catacombs and into new, unexplored spaces. Sure, several hundred rats would be killed, along with a few cats, but there were thousands more, not counting the mice.

The Reporter knew the public would be interested in the origins of the Speaker's discovery in his bathroom. But, he thought: Now is not the time. Now is the time for him to stay ahead of the developing story so the insatiable public sees his website as the go-to one for the latest eruptions. First, the Reporter needed to scan the media coverage and the audience feedback. He found it was journalistic bedlam. The rat invasion was such an off-the-charts story, without precedent, that it produced a riot of rumors, sneers, editorializing in news reports, satiric condescension, and wild cartoons. The right-wing radio talk shows hosts went ballistic even by their rather brutish standards. All their venom, scarcely suppressed in normal hours, exploded like a volcano. One host, in a tone of savage seriousness, urged an indefinite shutdown of Congress, saying that the rats could run the place better and not cost the taxpayers as much. The conspiracy boys were having a field day with their callers. Some opined that this was all a plot hatched by Pinko lawmakers who wanted to avert an upcoming tax cut debate favored by all red-blooded Americans. "It's all about distracting us and giving these critters some more vacation time," drawled a Texan caller. A letter-to-the-editor by a super patriot demanded that all American flags on the Capitol be taken down. "How can our beloved flag fly over buildings dominated by hordes of rats?" she wrote. One news headline, decrying the "mum's the word" posture of the lawmakers, read "Congress United Not to Talk: Rats Achieve the Ultimate Filibuster Closedown."

The Reporter always admired cartoonists as being the least restrained but most imaginative of his journalistic colleagues. He was not disappointed. One after another drew cartoons of the terror-stricken Speaker and Minority Leader in their bathrooms reacting to the officious rodents whose facial expressions conveyed a "What the heck is going on here?" message. A particularly good one showed an armada of weapons moving toward the Congress followed by (in the next panel) a group of rats dining on some spilled food, with one rodent speculating, "Do you think they'll use an F-35?"

The late night TV shows showcased a range of experts whose attempts at serious commentary produced even greater laughter from the audiences. A medical specialist in infectious diseases pondered the effect of rat bites on different parts of the human anatomy. When a psychologist was asked whether the Congressional buildings can ever be a place where young women would wish to start their careers, he replied, "Why did you single out young women?"

"Well," replied the host, "don't they have the most horrifying eeeek factor?" The audience groaned and laughed at the same time.

The mainstream press tried to cover the rampage as a serious obstruction of government, a health problem, and a foreign policy setback due to the disrespectful global press treatment. At the White House press briefing, reporters asked with whom the President was meeting. They reasoned emergency declarations are associated with emergency meetings. The Press Secretary said that the President is meeting with leaders of Congress and his national security and health teams.

"Toward what end?" exclaimed the reporter from the *Washington Toast*.

"Toward developing a rapid response with first responders to overcome the scourge and its contamination," said the Press Secretary.

"Are the State Department and the Department of Defense engaged at all here?" queried the reporter from the *New York Chimes*.

"They are on alert to detect any foreign powers trying to take advantage of our Congressional emergency and are ready to respond to any foreign attempts to turn a serious health problem into an object of caricature or lampooning. After all, there are plenty of rat problems in every country," asserted the insurgent Press Secretary. "Indeed, the French Parliament was overrun by rats in 1952, but nobody talks about that."

(In his mind, the Press Secretary was thinking of the global image problem that the rat invasion was causing. He couldn't say it this way, but the nation's image was taken very seriously by the DooLittle Administration, especially because the President's surname made him the butt of many demeaning jokes.)

The Congressional invasion of the rats was a difficult matter for the media to handle, despite its sensational dynamic. There was really no one to blame yet; there were no previous statements by politicians to show any current hypocrisy; there was no grounds really to allow them to pit one politician against another—the rats were bipartisan in their nomadic ventures; there were no laws violated or unenforced; there were no human adversaries or enemies or fat-cat funders to produce endless questions.

The Reporter took in all these media forays and spent some hours digesting their aggregate significance as a way to help him determine where he should go next. He was not the mimicking type, obviously.

The All-Important Sheen

Meanwhile, the Speaker sat down to dinner with Regina and started his requested appetizer: stewed prunes in warm water followed by a dish of raisin bran soaked in warm milk with maple syrup. An ordinary dinner of flounder with pears, carrots, and mashed potatoes was the next course. While he was slowly consuming his meal, the Speaker wanted to talk, to say things that were on his mind that no one but Regina was allowed to hear.

"My dear, Regina, let me unburden myself further about my deep concerns over what is happening. As I mentioned, superficial appearances and images are extremely important to preserve, even though no one wants to admit or talk about this truism publicly. One reason for escalating this rodent mess to a Presidential emergency is to take away the laser of journalist attention that was fated to fall on me and the Minority Leader. Our strategic moves have taken the rat problem to a different, complex level of overall seriousness. This seems to be working so far, but it is fraught with the peril of boomeranging if and when the media starts going into the origins of this unforeseeable tumult.

"Look at the crucial psychological function of the sheen, the cover. No one ever visualizes George Washington on a toilet or Thomas Jefferson urinating or making love on top of a black slave. The masses learn from elementary school to see General George Washington on his white horse followed by the regulars of the Continental Army or to think of Thomas Jefferson posing with others signing the *Declaration of Independence* in 1776. When you think of the Crusaders to the humming of 'Onward Christian Soldiers,' you see them in proper regalia, not in a blood-fest, beheading thousands of Saracens in the aftermath of one victorious battle. When brutal, bloodthirsty, sadistic police for a murderous dictatorship show up for work each day, they are checked for clean, pressed uniforms and polished boots.

"Even to see us—members of Congress—in the gym or vigorously dancing perturbs this essential imagery of steadfast command, upstanding resolve and serious demeanor, regardless of what we are doing against peoples' interests and needs day by day. So when I see where the media is going, I'm deeply disturbed. Why, one fellow brashly asked an urologist on television, 'How serious would it have been had the black rat bitten off my balls, given that my wife and I are through having children?' You see where this whole thing is going. The reporters are taking us into a chasm of tastelessness and that sick pit is bottomless."

"Did you say 'bottomless,' dear," winked the irreverent Regina. "Never mind. I interrupted you. Keep going."

"Well, to finish, I see an emerging national mindset arising from the Presidential emergency that can grow and will end up undermining our essential personal vanities that, so effectively, shield us from the masses. By playing this so big, I may have created a monster, a Frankenstein.

Meet the Press is coming up Sunday and I have to go to my study and think long and hard about my presentation."

"Any dessert, dear?" Regina asked.

"Yes, sweetheart, bring me a bowl of those freshly picked figs with coffee," he said.

The Experts Weigh In

At an undisclosed location, around a large conference table, sat the top-level military, national security, and infectious disease officials. They were ordered by the President *not* to leave the premises without an immediate, comprehensive action plan. He added that they already have the resources, the knowledge, the authority—they just needed a plan that better work and work fast! "This is not foreign policy," he snapped knowingly.

The top Antiterrorism Chief opened the deliberations with a PowerPoint presentation in real time. Using the buildings' surveillance systems, he showed them the entire Capitol Hill complex and, room-by-room, one could see the little mammals scurrying around or leaping from one place to another or gnawing on hard and soft objects. Some appeared motionless, seeming to sense danger. They were right. The delivered savage cats were making their presence known and had already crushed the bones of rodents they caught. As opposed to these active characters, the Capitol Police seemed to all be routinely looking at their smartphones, oblivious to any need to be alert, now that the legislators and their staff have fled.

"As you can see, my colleagues, the scene is an unusual one, to put it mildly," declared the Chairman of the Joint Chiefs of Staff. "The rats now have occupied all spaces and then some. Meanwhile, the mice sense opportunity as well as peril and are increasing in numbers. But there is so much food that they're not fighting each other.

"As the PowerPoint suggests, our first cognition should be to not overreact. Overreaction plays into the hands of these little terrorists—

and that's why they are attacking the space of innocent civilians with their many pathogens. It is equally imperative not to underreact given the time pressure we're operating under.

"Let us first get an up-to-date report from the Catman as to how the cats are doing.

He turned to the feline specialist, who said, "Thank you, boss. First, there are not enough cats and they are starting to fight each other. They have mean genes.

"Second, after they kill and chew on two or three rats, they get lazy and sit down sleepily. Apparently there is only so much action they can take."

("Like male lions," mumbled one attendee to herself.)

"My judgment is they're not the solution to the dilution of the rodents."

"Most interesting, Catman," noted the anti-terrorism honcho. "We'll accept your candid conclusion and move to the higher plane of technological response. Let us hear from Chemical Warfare Man."

"Thank you, Chief," said this specialist, who had a gas mask dangling casually around his neck. "I believe the only way to exterminate and make their successors unable to return is with our new gas: Rodblot. The manufacturer of Rodblot claims it is harmless to humans who come into a sprayed space, harmless after a forty-eight-hour interval, while the polluted air is flushed out. But rodents are extremely gene-sensitive to Rodblot. Specifically, rodents of the rat and mouse gene type.

"So the plan is that we advance on the Congress with giant hoses, spraying Rodblot into every square inch and crevice and pipe of that exalted architecture right down to the catacombs. The gas expands very quickly," he added.

"Where else has it been used?" demanded the Infectious Disease Man across the table.

"This will be its premiere, real-world application, the company told us," responded the Chemical Warfare Man proudly. "These rats will be just as good as lab mice for our purposes."

"What? What?" shouted the Infectious Disease Man, pounding his fist on the table for emphasis. "You are planning to use five hundred and thirty-five of the most important people in our country, and their staff, as guinea pigs?"

"Of course not," a red-faced Chemical Warfare Man II replied. "Rodblot has actually been tested on guinea pigs as well as assorted reptiles and mammals, including one great ape. The short-term findings on its killing power are reassuring, according to the manufacturer."

The Chief interjected testily: "Chemical Man II, your 'short-term' Rodblot is utterly too risky as a response to what should be a modest challenge. That is, if my associate, Infectious Disease Woman, agrees that the pathogens can readily be brought under control." He glanced down the table to one of his disease experts, "What say you?"

Infectious Disease Woman had the confidence that did not suffer fools gladly. She was glaring at the brash Chemical Man II but quickly composed herself to say that pathogens on rats can thrive only on contact, except for bubonic plague fleas which are not operative here. So long as there are no touching of fluids, no bites and no contamination of anything edible, the situation should be amenable to normal control. "So I must say," she added, "I approve the evacuation. We can wipe them out handily because, so long as the rats are not exceedingly hungry, they will not be behaving in an unusually aggressive manner or take risks about where they roam."

The Chief was relieved and said so. He then asked, "What do the professional rat exterminators think about the scale of this challenge?"

The Liaison Woman answered that they were recommending deploying large numbers of rat traps and rat poison as well as sealing any holes, crevices, or cracks. It's what they have always done, with satisfactory results, although they did feel a little bit overwhelmed and, certainly, the company that has been retained felt it lacked adequate man (and woman) power for the task ahead. When asked, company spokespeople said it will take a thousand workers—front and back-up— to do the job in about twenty days.

"Twenty days!" exclaimed the Congressional Rep, throwing up his hands. "That would wreck us. Don't you realize that our standing in the polls is plummeting by the hour from this media frenzy? As one libertarian wag put it, "The flight of the rats from the rats" is dominating the small talk of the people, folks who never knew the names of their own senators before. Even before this, there was a historic plunge in esteem and respect for the Congress as an institution. Now its members, not just the institution, are being held in low regard. Why, already there are rumors afoot of marches on Congress to throw dead rats at our edifices. Each marcher, it is said, will have a little sign around his or her neck signifying anger over some supposed bad deal or sell-out by their representatives. Who knows what other high-visibility farces and clownishness are on the horizon? Twenty days are an eternity and—if I may continue to mix metaphors—one with a long tail.

"He's also throwing in god-awful puns," Liaison Woman muttered.

"You've got to do better," wailed the Rep, sounding almost pathetic.

The Chief felt baffled but did not show it. He had never encountered such foes in his career. He looked over to the CIA Man and asked if he had a solution.

"No, sir, this problem is above all our pay grades and outside all the specialties at the agency. All we have found is that it doesn't seem to be a conspiracy, either domestic or from North Korea, China, Cuba, or the Russians. And our top men say rodents don't have the intelligence to hatch a plot to bring down our government."

The Chief looked further down the table. "How about you, NSA Man? You got any ideas?"

"Well, sir, though we have the classified, 'throne room' conversations (and exclamations) arising from the first discovery of the rats in the toilet, I am afraid the rats have bested us by using their natural born encryption," he added smiling wanly and, to the Chief's mind, inappropriately, given the gravity of the situation.

The DC Police Chief and Fire Chief, along with DC's Rodent and Vector Control Division Director, were listening to these exchanges with quiet astonishment. Their thoughts ran along similar lines, all amounting to: "So this is what the 'best and brightest' can come up with. Nothing! We may as well let the traditional exterminating firms be given the funding and support to go after these rats the old fashioned way. We can brook no further delays unless some unknown genius comes up with a better way."

The Fire Chief voiced all three's opinion when he spoke up: "Given the difficulties that all of you are expressing, why not try crowdsourcing to get the best possible recommendations quickly? Just lay out the

Ralph Nader

problem and ask people to come up with ideas. The Internet is the world's greatest suggestion box."

The Fire Chief's suggestion was a nonstarter all around. Publicizing the problem and the experts' problem in finding a solution would be an admission that the government, with all its skills, had laid an egg. Everybody was thinking, *It's bad enough Congress is taking the abuse without including the Executive Branch.*

Not even considering the Fire Chief's suggestion, the Antiterrorism Chief asked for a show of hands of those who wanted to go with the expanded extermination attack on three shifts daily. All hands went up, except for that of the Infectious Disease Woman, who abstained.

The Task Force had gotten its marching orders and transmitted them to the President who, nonplussed over the absence of any high-tech remedies, nevertheless initiated the procurement of one thousand exterminators, who would start immediately. This meant signing contracts with a dozen firms who were told to work together, carve out their territories inside the Congress, and coordinate daily.

The People's Wrath

Not a moment too soon, for the rumors mentioned in the war council were not far from the truth. The country's people were arousing like never before.

A contingent from New York and New England, led by nurses and students, delivered a truck load of "Wall Street Rats" with the sign explaining that they would obviously be welcomed by the Congress that had refused to pass a Wall Street speculation tax, such a sales tax would have provided $300 billion a year that might have been utilized to provide healthcare and reduce the student loan burdens. Millions of postcards were being sent showing one giant black rat on the Capitol Dome with a sign saying, "You Didn't Listen to Them—The People—But Now You're Going To Listen To Us." This was only a sliver of the corrosively critical anthropomorphism attributed to the rats and their imagined political agenda. They had become the voice of the public! Little statuettes of Blamer, Melosay, and Clearwater, wearing crowns upon which lolled a pompous rat, were selling like hotcakes. Poster art rose to new heights of imaginative, symbolic, and real-life portrayals of what was increasingly being called the perfidious "Withering Heights" of Washington, DC.

The calendar was filled with non-stop street action: rallies, soapbox speeches, marches, and sit-ins at zoos where the protesters said the rats should be given luxury cages as reward for their heroic takeover. The media couldn't have enough of it. Ratings soared and increasing print, radio, and TV time was being devoted to what was making a very deep impression everywhere. Protests—across the country, red state, blue state, north, south, east, and west—were moving into mobilization stages with overdue specific demands for justice, fairness, and participation *qua* citizens replacing control *qua* wealth as the *sine qua non* of government functioning. And, the most ominous sign of all for incumbents: there were early indications of candidates, holding the same beliefs as the protesters, readying challenges to the lawmakers in the upcoming primaries.

Petitions were circulating on the Internet demanding the members go back to their jobs regardless of the rat infestation. Millions of workers show up every day at jobs far more dangerous. They don't cower in fear. If they did, they would have their pay cut or be fired by their bosses. The petition pointed out that Members of Congress were getting paid while they stayed home in bed. Outrageous! These petitions contained common left/right demands—the kind that really scare politicians.

Speaker Blamer Searches His Soul In Public

Speaker Blamer was really worried by back-home pressures from his constituents. He sensed they were not going to burn out as easily as had the fire behind many weekend anti-war marches he had been initially scared by years ago. The rat explosion was simply too visceral, too inviting of sneering public indignation.

Ralph Nader

Sunday morning, Speaker Blamer's driver arrived to pick him up for the 9 am TV taping for *Meet the Press*, which would be played nationwide at 10:30 am. Woodcock Toad, the legendary interrogator, had been prepping for this hour non-stop since Speaker Blamer agreed to come on. For the full hour, the usual format was to be tossed aside. There was no time for the insipid commentator panel of cautious but very vocal reporters and syndicated columnists.

Speaker Blamer arrived at the entrance to the spacious NBC headquarters on Nebraska Avenue only to encounter outside a gaggle of television cameras and reporters who began throwing questions at him while he hastened to the studio door. "No comment, have to go," he told them. "Watch the show." He kept his head up, his posture erect, and his visage confident, using his most impressive baritone voice to brush them off. "Dignity, Bearing, Image," he silently repeated to himself.

Once inside, he was ushered into the green room, which was replete with fruits, drinks, and bakery delights. From there, he was taken next door to make-up, where a true artist of the form made him look almost regal. Back in the green room, he was greeted by Woodcock Toad (nicknamed Woody) and told that the whole hour was being devoted to the Congressional rat invasion and how the government and the American people were reacting to this unprecedented Congressional Emergency. There was a small number of people comprising a studio audience, Blamer was informed, but all the questions would come from Woody.

Mr. Toad began the show with a three-minute introduction, discussing the closedown of Congress due to the rats, and spicing his comments with suitable clips of the evacuation scene and statements by some senators and representatives. Toad ended with a picture of a dozen rats scurrying merrily in various directions in a Congressional office.

Turning to the Speaker, the host launched his first question: "Speaker Blamer, the reliable dispatches of the Reporter tell us that the first rat intrusion was in your own personal bathroom and that you let out a screeching bellow when you saw a big black rat in your toilet just as you sat down to use it. Could you describe for our audience your first reaction, how this came to be, and what you have tried to do about it?"

Speaker Blamer: "Mr. Toad, I never was one to look backward. All

I wish to say is that the rat invasion became Congress-wide and created this most unfortunate closedown, which was necessary to allow the exterminators to go to work. This is not about me."

Mr. Toad wouldn't be distracted: "But there are conspiracy theories being woven about why it started with your bathroom and why the first rat picked on your—err—you? Could you put these rumors to rest?"

Speaker Blamer said, stiffening ever so slightly, "Mr. Toad, I can't deal with rumors and the crazed delusions of plot-spinners. As far as I can see, it was just a random occurrence, the entrance into the plumbing of a fleeing rodent seeking food. Can't we talk about the larger picture here? For heaven's sake, the country is aroused over this closedown as never before."

Mr. Toad was not to be tamed: "Very well, Mr. Speaker, but is 'aroused' the right word here. That might suggest you are garnering the public's pity. Let me show you some of the clips from the demonstrators and a reading of the polls. Instead of sympathy from back home, you're getting an eruption of anger over the long-standing performance of Congress on behalf of the wealthy against the people. Look at these spontaneous rallies everywhere: Dayton, Austin, Miami, Providence, New York, Los Angeles, Denver, Peoria, Knoxville. They are even erupting in your home state of Indiana. And look at the polls, which show Congress's approval rating plummeting to single digits in red and blue states. What do you choose to say about all this?"

Blamer tried to turn the tables, "Mr. Toad, putting on my amateur psychologist's hat, I suspect the masses are vicariously identifying with the rats who, unlike them, have achieved an undreamed access to Congress and its members and have upset the place as never before. No foreign enemy or invader has come close, not even the British in 1812. So in their frustration, people are getting some glee and taking the opportunity to send all of us in Washington a message."

Mr. Toad shot back. "A message, Mr. Speaker? That's interesting." Toad scented news was about to be made. "Just what would that message be?"

Unbeknownst to the media, Blamer was anticipating a strong candidate emerging as a possible opponent in his next election, so he had decided to do what he could, though it would shock some of his fellow representatives, to steal this guy's thunder.

Ralph Nader

"Mr. Toad, to put it simply, the people are telling us to do in Congress what they sent us there to do—represent them—and stop this mad rush to raise money from commercial interests, which ends up making many legislators stand for these interests against the people. The public found a very effective way to send that message—and they are filling in the details by the day—and that is through mockery, derision, lampooning, satire, all with the abetting of a media that is very attentive to anything sensational. I don't need to tell you in the media—because you are the transmitters— that turning us all into a laughing stock is a devastatingly effective way to get our attention. It takes away our dignity, our presentation of self. So that's my two-minute psychological sermon. Next question."

Toad couldn't help but show surprise in his voice. "Mr. Speaker, you're flooring me. It is one thing for you to describe this mass arousal that is growing by the hour, but you, a conservative, seem to be acceding to its message. It's as if you are egging these malcontents on. Or am I getting something wrong here?"

Blamer was thinking that as he had started on this route he might as well go all the way, harking back to the teachings of his youth, which still had a faint resonance in the depths of his consciousness. "Mr. Toad, I've been around a long time. And I've seen and sometimes participated in, I say to my shame, a lot of sleazy deals. For me, very frankly, it is by the grace of God that I still have my testicles, in both senses of the phrase.

"I feel this dispensation to be a salvation of sorts, almost a divine inter- vention, which is telling me to heed my maker and to begin applying the teachings of Jesus, the Son of God. You know most of my colleagues go to their places of worship and leave their scriptural values there when they leave. I've decided that I must now take seriously the Ten Com- mandments, not as something we demand be placed in secular public places for ornamentation, but as words to live by. They don't know it, of course, but, if I'm right and other of my fellow legislators are feeling this same change of heart or, better said, are getting a heart, the way I am, then in their coming massacre by the exterminators, these little animals are dying for our souls. And if it took the rats to do this, instead of our own consciences, our pretensions, our own knowledge of the awful depri- vation, exclusion, devaluing, and disrespect of our people back home, SO BE IT!" Whereupon the Speaker bit his lip a bit for emphasis.

Back in the Speaker's home, Regina sucked air spasmodically—in delight. Years ago, she had given up hoping for this moment of epiphany to come, one she knew lay latent for so long in Reginald's inner self. This was the first time in memory she could recall watching him on TV when she actually waited for more of his words with pleasure.

A thousand on-looking reporters and commentators weren't waiting; they were filing their stories on their laptops, gulping their drinks and trying to clear their heads, hardly believing what they had been hearing. The instant reports reflected their political inclinations. "Speaker Blamer Capitulates to Rats" headlined a reporter for Faux News. "House Speaker Glows in Epiphany Moment" wrote a freelancer for a religious magazine. They had only time to quote his words verbatim. The commentary would come later after the conclusion of the program.

Mr. Toad announced a commercial break, adding needlessly, "Stay with us!" The Nielsen was registering an audience increase of 150,000 viewers per minute!

Blamer Still Telling It Like It Is

After the break, Mr. Toad, who had thrown out all his notes, resumed, "Mr. Speaker, I have to be blunt. How do you square your declared religious principles with your steadfast, long-standing opposition to raising, or what some call restoring, the federal minimum wage, a move which is supported by about eighty percent of the American people?"

"Mr. Toad, let me play amateur psychologist again," he began. "Humans are very often of two workings, having an inner and an outer person. Now you and the nation's public are seeing the Speaker's authentic inner person. I am in the process of casting off my parasitic external self, maintaining only the few positive qualities linked to that self, and merging it with my true, inner self. Put that all together and you see a humble servant of the Lord.

"Perhaps you are used to hearing empty words from me. No more. On the reopening of the House of Representatives, I will put forward a bill to take the frozen minimum wage, this cruel and unnecessary chokehold on thirty million of my fellow human beings, to $15 an hour. This will almost reflect a forty-six-year inflation adjustment and a double productivity rate. Think about this. The latter means that, due to automation and streamlining of the company's operations, one Walmart worker today does the work accomplished by two Walmart workers in 1968. I think the CEO of Walmart can tolerate such a raise—much of which will be spent in Walmarts anyway—inasmuch as he makes $12,000 an hour along with getting extraordinary benefits and company-paid luxuries."

At this moment the watching media went into high gear collectively screeching out or trumpeting, depending on political stripe, the Speaker's message, which was, as one put it crisply in a headline: "Speaker Tosses the Bosses to Make Up the Worker's Losses." Inside the Beltway commentators speculated that his Republican Party members would be tossing the Speaker on their return. But outside the Beltway in American's cities, towns, and rural centers, those commentators with a feeling for the popular pulse said the grassroots' *will of the people* was responding to Blamer's remarks with a roar, shaking both the leader and rank and file of Congress to their boots.

Much as he liked Blamer's chutzpah, Toad was skeptical about Blamer's claim that he could really accomplish much by taking a hard charge at Congress. He prodded, "This is remarkable, Mr. Speaker, do you believe you can bring along your Party which has been opposed to any minimum wage increase for years?"

Mr. Speaker waxed lyrical: "Yes, I do. You know a famous poet, I think it was Shakespeare, said, 'The times they are a-changin'.' Many of my fellow representatives tell me they have been feeling the heat from back home for over a year. As one gentleman told me, 'Walmart workers who call themselves conservatives are not bamboozled enough by their own ideology that they will follow its teachings and *not* take overdue dollars to put food on the table for their families.' You know, Mr. Toad, I'm coming to feel the wealth of Wall Street is no match for the will of the people once it's expressed vigorously. The few only can rule the many when the many are asleep without an alarm clock. Well, the rats have given them the alarm clock. Talk about a Black Swan event!"

Toad was still trying to get on handle on Blamer's shocking turn-about in perspective. "Mr. Speaker," he said, "let's explore the political fallout that will result from your stand this morning. Can you give us some idea of what you see as happening in the coming weeks, with the extermination period and the resumption of Congress?"

Blamer didn't see himself as a prophet, as he told Toad. "I am not prone to speculation. One reason I wear a vest is to keep myself close to it. All I can tell you is: Keep an eye on the many-faceted upheavals and outcries that are occurring around the country. That's where I think a new chapter is being written. This may be a period of American history where the people *lead* and the leaders *follow*. It won't be the first time. That's what occurred in the first intense American Revolution against King George III and his edicts. It began non-violently in 1774 with the farmers in central and western Massachusetts, who were starting mass protests before Boston, Lexington, and Concord got into the act and seized the credit. I would guess that so many outbursts and creative pushes, Mr. Toad, are going to come out from people—so long having given up their sovereignty in a kind of prolonged American serfdom—that those of you in the media, even working around the clock, won't be able to keep up with."

Blamer's Dirty Secret

At that moment, there was a real black swan, or better, brown swan event, which seemed poised to derail Blamer's credibility. It came over the news that one of the workers clearing the rats, mice and droppings from the Speaker's private bathroom discovered all kinds of dried shit and strips of toilet paper in the Speaker's bathtub's drain—of all confounding places. This bawdy tidbit was instantly blasted all over the Internet, all over the regular media, and in seconds became a viral monster responded to with uncontrollable laughter. It was picked up on and rebroadcast by the thousand reporters and commentators watching the show. Even the producer feeding instructions and suggestions to Mr.

Toad's earplug lost self-control as he read the news, breaking out in hissing hilarity, which he tried, but failed to suppress.

The commentary spread across the generations. "The Speaker fled his toilet and was crapping in his own bathtub!!?? Oh, how gross!" exclaimed a million teenagers. "Pretty damn innovative," shrieked two million millennials. "You have to grant he was practical, at least the Speaker chose the bathtub over the sink," joked three million baby boomers. While the elderly multitudes could only say, "Is that so? Well, what do you know that don't show?"

Mr. Toad got the news the minute he looked down on his smartphone. The only human in America who didn't know was the Speaker who, with folded hands and head held high, awaited the next question.

Mr. Toad got his job as host of *Meet the Press* partially because of his reputation for quick reaction, a skill honed during a three-year stint at the White House, where he regularly sparred with the press secretary and occasionally with the President. But never had he faced a challenge like this during a live program, one which he had learned at break was registering the biggest ratings in the storied history of this television network institution. His neurons were blasting away furiously in the nanoseconds he had at his disposal while he formulated his next question.

To gain a minute, he showed people demonstrating and in some cases encircling some local television buildings with placards demanding that all members of Congress resign and order special elections for a people's legislature.

At that moment, the producer, seeking to get Mr. Toad to put some rat-in-the-bathroom personal type questions to the Speaker, sent a comedian's joke to Toad's smartphone: "Why did the Speaker choose to shit in his bathtub instead of his sink?" Answer: "Because the Speaker couldn't jump high enough?" Mr. Toad was not amused, texting acerbically, "Enough with the bathtub humor. Leave me alone."

Keeping It Clean, For the Moment

Clip over, Mr. Toad resumed, much to his producer's chagrin, with a neutral question: "Mr. Speaker, what do you think of these demonstrators who are seeking a mass resignation of Congress and new elections?"

"Well, I think that is quite premature. They might wait to see if it is at all necessary when the Congress returns from its enforced vacation and takes up the new agenda I'm considering."

"What do you mean, Mr. Speaker?" Toad probed.

"When we return, my first order of business will be to meet with my Caucus *in public* and call on them to join me in ending all DOUBLETALK.

"Most will know what I mean, but, just in case some are ignorant, I'll offer them a few examples. Some supported the oddly named 'Water Rights Protection Act,' which would end federal authority to maintain minimum stream flows for fish and wildlife and give skiing companies more control over their use of water on public lands. How's that for protection? Or how about the 'Restoring Healthy Forests Act,' which would allow more cutting in our national forests by companies, who would be able to chop away without public input or environmental review. Then there's the 'Reducing Regulatory Burdens Act' that would let agribusiness dump regulated pesticides into navigable waterways without having to get a permit. Or take this DOUBLETALK gem: the 'Ensuring Public Involvement in the Creation of National Monuments Act,' which would hamstring the President's century-old authority to help protect millions of acres of public land. All these fabricated bills actually passed the House of Representatives but were blocked in the Senate. God help us if they ever come up with the 'Human Protection Act.'

"And you know, Woody," Blamer said, getting a little avuncular, "doubletalk always goes hand in hand with double-dealing and hypocrisy. If you want to see the hypocrisy practiced as a fine art look to the deficit-reduction crowd. We, and, to my shame you have to include the old me in that number, are always demanding that the federal deficit be slashed. Yet while Congress uses chainsaws to cut welfare benefits,

Ralph Nader

it uses a toenail clipper on the Pentagon's budget, even refusing to drop projects and domestic bases that the Pentagon itself wants eliminated. We keep cutting the IRS's modest budget to the bone so that it doesn't have the personnel to find and collect the *$400 billion* a year, one year, in unpaid evaded taxes. Is that counterintuitive or what? It's certainly a dumb way to swell the deficit. If the boys and girls want more examples of unneeded bloat that can be unfunded and necessary services that benefit the people, that need more money, my staff will flood them with examples. That's something that will be done in full public view in front of the Capitol Hill Press Corps."

"Mr. Speaker, many of your colleagues are watching you say all this *live on national television*. What do you think they are thinking about doing?"

"Mr. Toad, right now, while some may be thinking about the reactions of their deep-pocketed supporters, I'll wager most're thinking about what the common people watching this program are thinking about them. Then they'll start rethinking. Maybe, as an aid to their musings, I can suggest they also get a copy of "the golden rule" and text it to the Chairman of the House Rules Committee with the words: 'This is the way to simplify your daily work.'"

Mr. Toad interrupted the Speaker's flow of words. "But why are you singling out the Chairman in particular?"

"Because, as you know, this 'Chairman Nyet,' as some critics call him, is considered the hardest of the hardliners."

"Mr. Speaker, you seem to be fully at ease with what I will call your new world view, but I've never heard you express even a trace of this before. Don't you think this was too sudden, that you might have discussed this at least with the inner circles of the Republican Party, giving them a heads-up, so to speak?"

The Speaker's exuberance seemed to know no bounds. "Woody, when the time comes for an out-of-date totem pole of political structures to fall, it falls fast, just like the Soviet Union fell. To let the debris flake and then slide off at an increasing rate, bringing the structure to a slow collapse, is destabilizing to our national security. There is the need for a clean break to see if redemption is possible."

As the show was almost over, Mr. Toad came up with a tremendous finish, which might even allow him to go into overtime. "Mr. Speaker, I've just been informed that a small crowd of Washingtonians is gathering in front of our gated NBC Building, including numerous members of the media eager to ask you their questions. You can see them on the monitor. What do you say we go out to greet them and take questions? Don't worry. NBC's security team will keep some semblance of order and quiet. If things get overwhelming, we'll just come back into the studio."

As the Speaker nodded his head indicating the move outside was agreeable to him. Mr. Toad added, "We'll keep showing what's going on around the country and some cartoons for our viewing audience as we move outside."

"Okay by me, Mr. Toad. Just keep the din down so we can hear."

Taking It to the Streets

As they left their seats and moved down the corridors of the NBC offices, cameramen and assistants moved with Toad and the Speaker to the front entrance.

Once outside, Mr. Toad changed hats from being an interviewer to being a stage manager. He looked out at the crowd pressing toward them. "Hello everyone. Let's first hear from members of the media and then our reporters will take some questions from other audience members. Please, make your questions crisp as there is not much time left."

The first questioner was a female TV journalist, "Mr. Speaker, people always say, 'it takes two to tango.' My question is: What about the Senate—a notoriously independent body? Will they get behind your plan?"

The Speaker replied, "The rats will take care of them too. I expect smooth relations in our rapid response to the folks out there in the country."

That seemed overly optimistic to many of the listeners, but rather

Ralph Nader

than argue that point with him, the next journalist, a male radio reporter, asked for details. "Mr. Speaker, can you come up with an agenda as comprehensive, as varied and as straightforward as the people are insisting on in their mounting sense of liberated power?"

This radio guy had been reporting on the protests around the country, which inspired his query.

"Rest assured," the Speaker explained, "the agenda I'm proposing has been around for a long time. It could be called 'Catching up with Canada or Western Europe,' or going back to the Populist Party platform of 1912 or parts of the 2002 Texas Republican Party platform or, to move even further back, to some writings of Adam Smith or, to move back millenniums, the scriptures of the great religions."

The Speaker saw a sly grin on the reporter's face.

"I'm not being facetious," he told him. "The modern forms are on paper, written by some of our enlightened legislators here, and at the state level. They are in neglected GAO reports and in the studies by the Congressional Research Service and our universities and citizen groups. Also you can find them among existing best practices of local, state and federal governments or in the better corporations like the Interface Company in Atlanta, Georgia, or Pantgonia in Ventura, California. The challenge of finding a viable agenda is the least of my worries."

At this point, Mr. Toad decided to mix things up a bit by allowing a citizen to ask a question. The man queried, "Mr. Speaker, what then are your bigger worries?"

Now it was the turn of the Speaker to wear a wry smile. "Whether we can move fast enough before the Congress is torn down as was the Bastille in 1789."

Mr. Toad was shaken by this allusion and jumped in. "The Bastille? Surely, Mr. Speaker, you're not anticipating violence, are you?"

The Speaker was quick to backpedal. "No, of course not. I was being metaphorical. After all, the Bastille wasn't literally torn down on the spot. I was referring to an old saying about archaic, ossified institutions— whether public or private—'If they don't bend, they are going to break.' I assure you, Congress will bend or it's history." The Speaker paused then, and as an afterthought, added, "This is an election year, you know."

Mr. Toad identified the next questioner, a black woman standing with her assembled husband and little children. "Our race knows about revivals—like Reconstruction—and what can come after, groups such as the triple-K Southern Redeemers who were depicted so lovingly in the racist film *The Birth of A Nation*. Have you thought about any backlash and who would make up it its adherents?"

Mr. Toad was disappointed to hear, via text, that the network would not extend his program any longer. "Wow, that's a heavy good one. Unfortunately, although it would be great if you could speak at length on this topic, you've got two minutes left for your reply, Mr. Speaker."

"A profound issue, Madame," the Speaker began, then admitted, "I haven't really given it much thought, except to believe that everybody wins when America catches up with justice. Sure, those short-sighted barons of Wall Street and Houston will have to give up significant power, but isn't it possible they will be smart enough to know that, in the long run, they'll be better off? The change will make them better behaved too.

"You don't have to read Aristotle's *Politics* to see that democracies are always more prosperous for everybody than plutocracies in part because of the people having more spending power from higher incomes and everyone being willing to invest more due to the society's greater stability. Some of the rich may grasp this, but the ruling one percent usually includes some really rich, really greedy people who don't consider society's overall prosperity but act to worsen inequalities and divide the people into warring factions.

"Maybe my confidence is misplaced. But I'm foreseeing the Congress, prompted by the rat onslaught, will awaken as I have. I imagine this awakened Congress will NOT try to divide and rule and generate class warfare, and will work for everybody except, in the short-run, the global corporations, who will have to toe the new line of fair play. After all, they are supposed to have been chartered into existence by governments to be the servants of the people, not their masters. My key message goes out to the common woman and man, not to my colleagues in Congress. It is: Keep building reasoned, serious pressure on all legislators. Then you can direct your representatives from a position of knowledge and power. After all, aren't we supposed to be your public servants? So, shouldn't you, the people, be setting the agenda?"

Ralph Nader

Mr. Toad had the last word. "Mr. Speaker, this has been an outstanding *Meet the Press* thanks to you and people out there. We hope to have you back very soon. And, for now, on behalf of NBC and my colleagues, if it's Sunday, it's *Meet the Press.*

Roars erupted in neighborhoods around the country. The thousand reporters and commentators rushed to write their stories and opinions. The headline experts smacked their lips as they unloaded some doozies for the morning papers and the weekly magazines. The sensationalist media got its sensations.

The Story Behind the Story I:
Workers Do Their Utmost

On the following Monday morning, the Reporter was not where all the others were: ditto-heading and rehashing their accounts of the Big Sunday Story. He was assembling a groundbreaking batch of fresh revelations into a dispatch that would show the story behind the story and, incidentally, prove once and for all that he was and would remain *numero uno!*

Spending day and night around the congressional complex—he had no trouble seeing what was going on at night as there were Kleig lights everywhere—the Reporter mixed with the workers who were coming in and out or sitting in trucks waiting in line to deliver or take away equipment and materials. He also casually approached them as they sat in nearby fast-food eateries. Here is what he put in his latest dispatch:

> Reliable sources at the rat extermination sites say that the number of rats and mice is increasing. This appeared hard to explain until this reporter learned that rats communicate to one another over wide ranges. Faraway rats were told there was plenty of food and spaces to hide in the Congressional complex. It also turns out that these rats have discovered and gnawed through emergency stores of food hidden all over the Con-

gress, put there in the old Cold War days of civil defense. The word spread and the rats starting coming over from Executive Departments in the vicinity, then further away from the slums of Anacostia and the underground tunnels of Washington, DC's aging water/sewage, subways, and other infrastructures.

To be sure, the rat slaughter has commenced in earnest. But rats are accustomed to seeing dead rats, eliminated by predators, diseases, and man-made disasters such as fires. Rats also cannibalize themselves, especially as they need much nourishment growing up from infancy to adulthood in just a few weeks. Moreover, rats always come back—sooner or later.

Other developments are causing new worry among the extermination teams and their health/safety overseers. One rat bite of a worker, who carelessly stuck his hand in a crevice, turned out to test positive for rabies. Two other workers have come down with a cough that may be associated with rat fleas. The health specialists were taking no chances. They ordered cessation of the work until all laborers were outfitted with hazmat suits from top to bottom. This order, which will be announced tomorrow, according to spokespeople for the cleanup, will delay the job for at least three days. In addition, to get a fix on possible health hazards, bottles holding sample rat fleas have been flown under super-secure conditions to the Centers for Disease Control in Atlanta, Georgia.

Despite these problems, the morale of the exterminators is quite high, according to interviews by this reporter, in part because they feel excited to be part and parcel of the biggest news story in the country. This is a marked contrast to their normal situation where they work in the shadows, unheralded and unknown. They are not used to being described in the same glowing terms used, for instance, for courageous firefighters. Second, they too heard the jokes. The late-night TV skits and cartoons are circulating on their smartphones as well. One late-night comedian, Wally Wholebear, went viral with this offering—"Well it took the rats to make the pompous politicians in Congress have some skin in the game." So, they can appreciate the rats are, in their unknowing way, doing a patriotic service by getting the public aroused. Of course, this hardly stops the workers from doing their utmost to eliminate the rodent scourge. From my contact with them, I can say the American people can rest assured that these men and women are skilled and dedicated to delivering a rat-free US Congress on time!

The Reporter filed his dispatch and told his editor that he was leaving town because that was where the next big story was developing. The Editor smacked his lips in anticipation as he opened the Reporter's FYEO file.

The Story Behind the Story II: Congress on the March

The Reporter had actually turned in two stories. The other one answered the question: "Where did all the Congressional lawmakers go when Congress was rat-closed?" He found, through his many calls, leads, and informants, that about a third of them went out of their home districts, usually out of their state for vacations in the Caribbean and sunny spots elsewhere. A few dozen accepted invitations to attend business conventions or golf tournaments at resorts. About sixty of the lawmakers went on taxpayer-paid junkets to study parliamentary systems abroad with Europe being the prime destination, particularly going to countries that had fine restaurants. The rest went home to do politicking. The headline read: "Congressional lawmakers vamoose for water holes of the rich, famous and powerful during Rat Recess."

The Reporter winced a little at such titular sensationalism, but he understood the news business. He also guessed that he would be the leader of the pack. As soon as his story was available, the rest of the press picked up and ran with the disclosures. The opinion-makers were not far behind. The bellowing radio talk show hosts were in high gallop, led by the growling, Tush Limba. The websites of the lawmakers had long since broken down and their phones were not answering, which further outraged the citizenry who were already aroused by angered radio hosts and the innumerable blogs. New domain names were registered, which were too inflammatory for the more discreet press to mention, except for the more reserved ones such as "Make Congress Collapse," "Clearwater Crap-out," and "Congressional Medal of Honor for the Rats."

Tush Limba summed up the citizens' responses: "Say it to Melosay and Blamer and all of them: Get out."

A Movement is Born from Stony Beginnings

Protests rise and fall in the ether for the most part. They generally don't ripple out from the core group of concerned people who originate them. Experts on crowds attribute this to little planning, minuscule budgets, poor leadership, and the lack of focus which induces protest fatigue among the core before they make an impact. The core never convincingly answers the questions, "Just How Far Do the Majority of Our Fellow Citizens Want To Go and How Do They Expect to Get There?"

Another explanation for the lackluster showing of protest movements in this country is that American politicians, over the past twenty-five years, have learned to quietly dismiss big rallies, demonstrations, and even temporary "occupations," because they have gone nowhere. The lawmakers never consider them when making decisions. Remember, too, that in Washington, giant rallies, such as those against the Iraq War, for the environment or for a jobs program were traditionally held on weekends when neither the members of Congress nor the journalists were around. These crowds are lucky to get a picture in the Sunday newspapers. The lack of publicity curtails any impact they might have had. The smaller gatherings, even those by Veterans for Peace, get zeroed out completely, rating at best a paragraph squib deep in the paper.

One small interconnecting group that was gathering might have seemed destined to the same fading-away fate. Called Summon Our Lawmakers To Us, it was well-nigh invisible at first. Its quietude was not due to an inability to make an impact, but to its concentration, from the first, on planning intensity.

This group was not into venting, but engaged in laser-like, *in personam* lobbying. The members had seen that the most powerful, most successful lobbies on Congress—the ones that twist the lawmakers like putty pretzels—did not bother with demonstrations or marches. Corporate lobbies like the NRA and AIPAC (American Israel Public Affairs Committee) have most of the five hundred and thirty-five men and women doing their business right on Capitol Hill.

The Summons group—probably not yet more than two hundred and fifty varied citizens scattered throughout the country, including some, but not many, who were well-to-do—were not experienced lobbyists. They just were serious, calm, informed, and competent. You know the type when you see it.

What caught many of their attentions watching *Meet the Press* on that fateful Sunday was the Speaker's allusion to the first American Revolution of 1774 and its inception in the farmlands of Massachusetts. Promptly circulated by the more scholarly of their group was the book *The First American Revolution: Before Lexington and Concord* by Ray Raphael. This enlightening volume, based on many primary sources from those heady days, told the amazing narrative of determination, presence, self-restraint, and focus displayed by thousands of farmers who played a large part in getting the revolt going. What organized them was the sudden, monarchical displacement of their local governments and courts by King George III and his Tory henchmen, their power grab backed by a sizable garrison of Redcoats billeted in Boston.

The networker who initiated this Summons group, mostly via the Internet, was Doug Colebrook, a recently retired stonemason whose ancient craft he had mastered and practiced over forty years. Methodical to an extreme, he started as a quarryman splitting sheets of rock, moved on to becoming a sawyer cutting rough blocks into cuboids, and then learned how to be a banker mason in the workshops that shaped the various kinds of stones into those right for a specific building's design.

Doug was a serious history buff in relation to stone craft. His reading took him back thousands of years to all the famous works of stonemasonry, including the Egyptian Pyramids, the Parthenon, Angkor Wat, the Taj Mahal, Cusco's Incan Wall, the mysterious Easter Island and Stonehenge statues, and Chartres Cathedral. His respect for markers and context led him into studying the cultural and political history at the times of these ancient constructions.

When Doug read the first article by the Reporter, one about the stirrings of protest around the nation, he sensed an historic opportunity flowing from the existence of so many kinds of vast and vivid reactions from the populace. Up to this time, he had despaired of anything being done to radically reform the country, especially through the existing system, given the deservedly low regard in which the public held Congress and the way that towering institution had walled itself off from the very people who sent its members there.

Learning From Our History

Doug obtained *The First American Revolution* and read it in one sitting. What struck him was the way the farmers—often five hundred to one thousand of them—would quietly surround the home of the resident Tory—who was their neighbor—and ask to see him. Then three or four of the assemblage would step forward and ask the Tory to renounce his assignment as a local implementer of the King's usurpations. There was no threat of violence. The farmers were very careful not to give the King's men any excuse to label them a "riotous mob," inviting an assault from the disciplined Redcoats. There was, however, a promise that if the Tory did not sign a recantation then and there, his independent neighbors would shun him, the farmers not sell him any of their products. And—note this—they would not even use the Tory appointed court judges or their sheriffs to present their regular claims or grievances, thus making these new, captive institutions a dead letter.

The Tory really only had two choices in these towns and villages of central and western Massachusetts—either to recant or leave for Boston and its protective Redcoats. Hanging around was just not a comfortable option, though some Tories would sporadically come back to spend time on their property and then go back to Boston if things got too hot.

The stonemason was impressed with the ability of the farmers to turn out in such large numbers during a time when the population of Massachusetts was about two percent of what it is in the present-day census. The peer group's mutual understanding that they were all in the struggle together and that they all had to pick up the oars in the lifeboat instilled awe in Doug. And this was underlined for him as he thought of how hard it is today to get voters to the polls or citizens to town meetings or rallies.

A Plan Gels

As a stonemason, Doug was used to reflecting while working. Unlike the more finely detailed tasks of plumbers, electricians, and roofers, stone-masons can concentrate on their craft and also think of other things. For Doug, these other things had come to be sequentially thinking through a problem or a challenge. That is, he became adept at mental concentration. When he was younger, the necessity for this trait as part of an effective person's equipment was brought home to him when he heard a lecturer recount Isaac Newton's response to a guest who asked why he was so much more brilliant than his scientific peers. Newton denied his superior acumen, noting only that he could hold a problem in his mind longer than most.

So after hours of concentrated reflection, Doug came to the conclusion that it only took a small number of determined people, backed by geographically widespread voiced public opinion and wielding sound tactics and strategies to make history, that is, to make significant changes in the body politic. After all, he told himself, there were only five hundred and thirty-five of them in Congress and they had the immense authority and power, to steer the country one way or the other.

Doug began putting out, in both real and virtual reality and in a very conversational manner, his thoughts on the traits, skills, and experience that would be needed by those who would set out to bring together a tightly knit, purpose-driven association of latter-day patriots. He carefully followed up any responses via the Internet with lengthy personal phone calls, letters, or personal one-on-one discussions with those who were nearby. Carefully matching policy agreements with the requisite personality and character strengths, he came up with about three hundred and fifty persons whom he believed concurred with him and each other on a list of long-overdue redirections and reforms.

It was after just completing his list that he read the latest investigation of the Reporter. The findings were exciting. After a careful survey of all Congressional primaries, the Reporter listed the names of three hundred and ten registered primary challengers in the House of Representatives and twenty-eight in the Senate. These were serious challengers from the same party as the incumbent, presenting a very rare and serious situation for incumbents accustomed to easy victories from their safely gerrymandered districts. Immediate media devolution followed the Reporter's scoop as hundreds of follow-up stories by state and local reporters appeared, ones that meshed powerfully with the ever-mounting popular outbursts, demands, and corrosive humor transfixing the land.

To the rat-evicted members of Congress, the near future was truly getting out of hand, out of their control, and unpredictable. Perhaps, they worried, their temporary displacement from Congress by the pesky rats would become permanent once November rolled around.

Suggestions from the circle that Doug was assembling included one by a self-described "very rich old guy," printed in Tudor English on a scroll. The elder proposed the issuance of a formal summons by the voters to the two senators and representatives of each of their states, who would be asked to come to open town meetings, chaired by the people, who would directly present their agenda, sent earlier to the lawmakers to be studied, for discussion and response. Thus the website, summonourlawmakerstous.org.

Now Doug followed up by preparing summonses to both incumbents and their primary challengers at other town meetings to review their capabilities and receptivity for the august offices in the Congress. Delighted, the "very rich old guy" called Doug up and said he would pay the travel expenses for all the circle's members to gather at Chicago's O'Hare airport to take matters to a new level of range and intensity. Doug scheduled the meeting at a large hotel for ten days hence.

The Country on Fire

Meanwhile, the Reporter was filing his daily, ground-based reports on the variety of condemnations and demands proliferating throughout the country, going, in his words, "creatively and effusively open source. It's America 2.0!"

The Reporter continued in one of his more comprehensive stories:

> What is transpiring is a multi-layered rising—a controlled civic riot producing seismic jolts at a rapid rate, fueled by the energy of millions of unemployed, underemployed, retired people, and supplied by an expanding mainstream market for material, such as rat figurines, posters, DVDs, balloons, pennants, banners, fireworks that explode to form the shape of the rat, brand new rat merry-go-rounds at theme parks that sell "ratburgers" (made of beef), and fantasy videogames where the player became a rat hot on the heels of a pants-less politician. Add the constant booming tunes for every taste making fun of the members by name in rap, rock, and—note this—waltzes. Not to mention the new trend for people to dine in *Ratskellers*.
>
> In the smaller towns, parade permits are setting all-time records, and protests are bringing people in record numbers to business-hungry store-front merchants.
>
> To this reporter, it seems everybody has a favorite gripe or pet peeve against these politicians, whether it be an irritating phrase the solon uses, an unanswered communication, a perceived air of remote arrogance, a lack of caring for any non-elite person's

plight, or the legislators' cavorting with the Wall Street or Hollywood crowd. It's very trans-partisan, almost a global repudiation.

Covering several locations a day in his red, white, and blue minivan, the Reporter filled his columns with local color and depictions of vociferous characters with their outsized props. There was theater to be sure, including marches with pitchforks, tar, and feathers, but the Reporter didn't describe these scenes as particularly festive. There was anger, disgust aplenty, rather than playfulness. People were picking up on each other's good ideas. The grim *rumble* from the people—the last thing politicians wanted to hear—was growing daily.

Moreover, for the politicians, these rumbling seemed highly ominous. In East St. Louis, Missouri, a turnout of low-income workers held posters saying, "We Need a Living Wage . . . or Else!" The "or Else" tagline went viral and began to bookend dozens of demands for a responsive Congress. "Repair Our Schools . . . or Else!" "Close Down the Nukes . . . or Else!" "We Want Our Homes Back . . . or Else!" "End Hunger and Homelessness . . . or Else!" "Tax Wall Street and End Student Debt . . . or Else." "We Want Simple Medicare For Everybody . . . or Else." "Regulate the Big Boys . . . Not Us . . . or Else!" "Bring Our Troops Home . . . or Else!" And of course, "Pro-Life . . . or Else!" and "Pro-Choice . . . or Else!"

Panic in the Suites

The ultimatum nature of the phrasing and the open-ended ambiguity of "or else" brought shudders to the senators and congresspersons who bothered to monitor the rumble day to day. And more and more of them felt they had to monitor these suspect goings-on. The two senators and the numerous representatives in each state were really taken aback when, just as they were gearing up for their reelection campaigns, they saw their own pictures carried by the marchers, often with a large X across their portraits.

Ralph Nader

Other members, from what had been very safe districts, shrugged their shoulders thinking or hoping the tumult in the streets and over the airwaves, Internet, and phones would blow over. They consoled themselves by remembering that such had been the fate of previous uprisings. "Let them blow off steam," said one solon from Delaware to his spouse. "Delaware will always be owned by DuPont unless Exxon/ Mobil wants to buy it," he joked.

By this time, however, while some lawmakers were still able to make light of the situation, the hoary corporate bosses were not joking. Some of them were getting alarmed, especially top executives in their forties who grew up with the social media and could see how devastating to their reputations its frenzies could be. In the recent past, they'd seen how those on this media would pounce on a plutocrat who used, just once, any politically incorrect words. Whatever occupational immunity these big bosses had under their convenient laws, they weren't immune from the viral ire of a cascading wave that at this point seemingly had no boundaries and no vulnerability to burnout so long as mocking laughter was mixed with real, long-suppressed grievances, all stemming from the feeling that ordinary people just don't count in the bigger scheme for those who rule them.

Many of these corporate honchos were quick witted enough to know that counter-measures were demanded immediately.

In a skyscraper high over New York City, around a gigantic conference table sat a pretty good sample of the most influential corporate CEOs and their advisors. Behind them lined up along the three side walls (the fourth side was reserved for refreshments and snacks) was a herd of second bananas. Little did these executives and their hench-people know that there was a ringer in their midst. One of these bananas turned out to be the Reporter, wearing a simple disguise. He was attached to an executive who was told that his usual aide, Mike, was under the weather and Frank was substituting.

The Chairman gaveled the meeting to order.

"Well, ladies and gentlemen, no preliminaries. I want to ask you right out: Do you think we may be losing our team down on the Hill and, if so, are we likely to end up with the junior varsity rubbing their hands for our goodies that they've long been preparing to seize once the old geezers take their leave?"

A silver-haired magnate took the floor, "If I can clarify first what you expressed in rather flowery terms, I think you are asking whether what's 'bursting out all over,' to coin a phrase, is the real beginning of a movement for fundamental change or just a large bunch of folks venting their spleen in a temporary spasm? If that's the question, register my response as 'Nobody knows.' As Shakespeare once said, 'The answer is blowing in the wind.'

"In other words, this could go all the way or just be an unusual expression of spring fever, a sort of frat boy rampage, with a lot of prancing and dancing without the lancing. Like an updated medieval 'Feast of Fools,' the few days of licensed irreverence that allowed the serfs to relieve pent-up tensions."

The next speaker, a well-known mogul, had a white mane and a loud voice. "Is everybody talking in riddles today. Just what do you mean by 'go all the way?'"

Silver mane clarified, "You know, a People's Revolution followed by chaos, internal dissension, betrayals, persecutions, executions . . . all that. Read a little history. We saw it in France and Russia and Cuba."

There was a nervous shuffling of feet and scratching of heads around the mega-table as each titan imagined a different version of apocalypse, and what losses it would entail.

The red–haired Chairman forced the issue: "Let me have a show of hands. How many think this is for real, the start of something big, and bad for business?" He counted the hands that shot up. "And now how many think a rat-driven revolution is simply not in the cards and will soon blow over?"

In counting the hands, the Chairman was happy to see the reals were blown away by the "blow-overs." He was satisfied in that he, too, thought of all this hullaballoo as a flash in the pan with the rabble blowing off steam without stamina. Moreover, this vote meant they wouldn't have to engage in hours of counter-movement planning.

The Chairman put forth his assessment of the situation. "Well, given the imbalance of opinion around the table, I don't see much value into probing lots of hypotheticals or in trying to find a latent message in the roars of the bloviating multitudes or the paranoias of our lawmakers, who admittedly and understandably are a bit shaken by the rat invasion and the public's treatment of the Congressional expulsion with mirth and madness. What's important to us is that the bond and stock markets continue to be stable, as they still are, and that our global partners are showing no consternations, putting ever more of their surplus money into US Treasuries. You may be pleased to note that our monitors of thousands of signs, placards, and posters—for we are keeping close tabs on the developing situation—find that though some want to have Congress tax Wall Street, not one sign called for an end to our derivatives trading or the Fed's lubricating 'quantitative easing.' So far, our major cash-cows-of-cash-cows, our brilliantly speculating through tier after tier with people's money, remains in the shadows."

This last thought brought perceptible feelings of relief to the plutocrats.

Another magnate, a more down-home fellow, commented, "Sol, old pal, long as we're here, let's talk turkey. We need to take the opportunity of this disruption to see about how we can get more deregulation, lower taxes, and more government grants and guarantees. Our loyal incumbents will want our friendship more than ever, given their rodent-induced panic. We can put their paranoia to use if we handle this right."

The bosses chortled and murmured their concurrence, remarking admiringly that Old Down Home always had his eye on the main chance. The Chairman brought in plates of delicious cuisine and expensive spirits, which diminished the tensions commensurate with their accumulating consumption.

The Reporter left the conference room, descended several floors to a men's room, where he took off his mustache and wig while he took stock of his disappointment. Truth was he had been expecting to be on the inside of a proverbial cabal, which would be planning detailed political, media, and espionage-oriented responses to what was going on. Though generally having a modest notion of his own talents, he had a flight of fancy at the beginning of the meeting that this inside story would get him the Hurlitzer Prize. Not this time. His eventual report did create a stir just because it was from an inside, fly-on-the-wall perspective, but not because the exchanges he described were Machiavellian. All the moguls and magnates had said resulted in a combined posture of complacency and, "Let's wait and see."

The Reporter returned to his office in Washington to write this all down.

Politicians for Change Face Usurpers

The first week of Rat extermination having just passed, Speaker Blamer, Minority Leader Melosay, and Senate Majority Leader Clearwater met at Blamer's home at ten pm. This was being done on the QT, off the radar, and under cover.

In something of a generational turnabout, these older leaders were trying to get in front of a movement for fundamental change, but they had found, and this was why they were meeting, a group of younger heads were seeking to bring them down. The three had sensed the early signs of a palace revolt.

At this point it was evident mostly in the House but quite capable of spreading to the other body. A clutch of Young Turks were starting the blame game. They were saying that if Blamer and Melosay had not been so secretive about their own asses and the toilets visited by rats, the rodent infiltration could have been nipped in the bud before the creatures went wild, swarming upstairs from the catacombs. The Young Turks stoked each other's fires, talking each other into heaving expressions of outrage. They saw their careers, so carefully cultivated with sycophancy toward their bosses and donors, going down, not in flames over some principle or ideology or campaign contribution, but going down in the face of public DERISION. How ignoble. This infuriated them!

As the trio sitting at Blamer's house had learned, the Turks had started discussing how they could separate themselves from their erstwhile leaders and save themselves from what they had come to believe was an approaching from-the-ground-up tsunami, which would soon sweep away the ruling leaders of the Congress.

It wasn't easy for the Turks to figure out what to do. Not easy at all. So they kept meeting—all thirty-three of them—nervously absorbing each day's developments around the country and searching for a way out that would promote—not deep-six—them. For added secrecy, the Young Turks took to meeting away from the Congress, but even so, the trio had become privy to their plans.

Regina poured wine, setting down the bottle next to a neat display of well-regarded cheeses and nuts she had laid out for her husband's colleagues. She then sat with them in the Speaker's comfortable, electronically swept den-study.

Blamer opened the proceedings. "Welcome all. Please do not hesitate to indulge in Regina's repast. You know why I called this meeting. As if the rat invasion and the emerging revolt of the masses are not enough to preoccupy our days and nights, now we have a sprouting of Young Turks thinking about breaking the venerable rules of succession. I tell you this whole situation is wearing me out. What about you guys? Are you feeling some fatigue?"

Minority Leader Melosay was having none of that gloom. "I'm not tired, my friend, I'm invigorated by all this conflict. You know, Reginald, I'm of the school that if you can't stand the heat, get out of the kitchen."

"Or the toilet," Regina told herself.

"We have to look for or create a luminous arc of immediate, substantive possibilities that takes away the spotlight on everything that is worrying us," Melosay said rather eloquently. "We have to put forward a vision of what we wish to implement for our beloved country, taking things progressively ahead in many directions, but ones that fall well within our Constitutional authority."

Senator Clearwater, who had not achieved his rank by eschewing caution, threw in, "Do you think we have to go all the way at this early date, I mean, straight to the last resort, so to speak?"

To Clearwater's ears, Minority Leader Melosay was getting as testy as Blamer. She said, "If we wait, we lose; if we don't seize the moment, the moment will seize us personally and . . . it won't be good for the country."

Regina thought Melosay's pause made it seem like the country was an afterthought.

The Speaker, for his part, cast a quick glance at the rare-book Family Bible open on the side table, perhaps as a bracer to stiffen his resolve as he expressed his next thought. "You know, Marcy, I don't need any convincing that we need to take the country in a new direction. Ever since my Sunday appearance on *Meet the Press* I am a different man. When you speak of how we must make fundamental alterations in the polity, you are speaking to a new choir, or rather a liberated choir. But right now, I am a choir of one in my Party. I don't see anyone seconding my recently voiced opinion. My partisans have been totally mum for the past sixty hours since I downloaded my conscience and made Regina proud."

Regina smiled with a slight nod.

Speaker Blamer turned to Clearwater. "Senator, I also believe this rat thing has unleashed irreversible forces around the country. It is early springtime, universally recognized as the season for protests, and I've heard that there are numerous cause marches: students, minorities, wounded veterans, impoverished workers, foreclosed home owners, even concussed athletes and others, what we might call affinity groups, set to go as the weather gets warmer. I'm not talking about a single, one-time-only demonstration on the Mall, but a separate march daily, picking up adherents mile after mile, with excited media in tow as the protesters head for the *day's named legislators* on Capitol Hill. The demonstrators are making it very, very personal.

"And to top it all—something none of us would have expected—there are some billionaires ready and eager to fund, and speed up, the whole avalanche heading for our heads! I see not one but many 'perfect storms' of completely unforeseen dimensions that our years of political savvy have never had to visualize, contemplate, much less learn to confront. To add gasoline to the fire, your Socialist Senator Ernie Banders is quoted in *New Yak Magazine* as saying he favors such singular marches on Washington and is looking forward, with gusto, to speaking before them. He adds that the marchers intend to bring caged, pet rats with them. For heaven's sakes, this dreadful symbol lives on undeterred and seems striving for our internment! If we don't do something, these rats will be carved on our headstones."

Calming himself after that outburst, the Speaker went on enumerating the components of the rising movement. "This giant rumble is going open source and its adherents are coming up with refinements that are like a thousand deadly cuts. Why, something called a people's bakery out of Kalamazoo, Michigan, is selling some juicy concoction in the shape of heads and torsos looking exactly like each member of

Congress. These tasty tidbits are to be fed to the rats during the course of the marches!!! Egads!"

"I'd rather be burned in effigy," groaned Senator Clearwater, "than be a witness to such lowly indignity—ugh, just *ugh*, and another *ugh*!"

At that moment, Melosay's smartphone, programmed to bell when a news break required her instant attention, rang out. She pardoned herself and read the missive from her confidential assistant Livinia:

"Ms. Melosay, the Reporter has struck again, exposing the meetings of the Young Turks plotting against the Speaker. It is just now coming across the wires. In some detail, I might add, but nothing we didn't know. Now the world will know."

Ms. Melosay turned and, without comment, read aloud the message. In response, the Speaker blanched and the Majority Leader of the Senate clenched his jaw.

The Speaker did see this as an opportunity to drive his point home. "This just gives more urgency to our conversation. You both saw my preliminary list of reforms on *Meet the Press*. I know you would approve, Marcy. What about you, Senator? Where do you stand?"

"From what I recall," said Senator Clearwater, "you spoke for the majority of the people. You might call it a big left/right super-majority. Things like union rights, better welfare, and so on are programs the folks in Western Europe would recognize since those amenities have been part of their lives for many years. So, in a phrase, and as I see it, 'No Big Deal.' Not that many of our fellow elite would characterize it like that. Even so, I'm sure you had other items on your mind, maybe even more fundamental changes, which there was no time to talk about."

The Speaker nodded: "You've read my mind on that one. Of course, there are other essential alterations that I have in mind, but some of them are reforms of Congress and the electoral system that don't 'sound-bite' and would register in listeners' minds as dull and uninteresting even if I had more time to outline them.

"But we're meeting now because of this Young Turk bubble-up, so let's focus on that for a minute. You know where they are coming from. This is a group of hardcore, conservative-feigning corporatists, elected when voter turn-out was at the lowest in the century and people were thoughtlessly biting their own noses to spite their own faces. These extremists are still oblivious to what's been going on in the country in recent days or, if they are paying attention, they think it is just a lot of hot air blowing from the hinterlands, which will cause a momentary temperature ripple and then blow out to sea. Either way, these Turks are a problem inside a puzzle and hard to take apart . . . or take down. Any ideas?"

Ms. Melosay speculated: "You could play the victimized statesman role. Make them *look* as if they are ungrateful jackals, viciously snapping at the heels of the man who had conferred innumerable benefits on them, besides their being out of touch with the American people, as the daily polls are demonstrating. This has to be done with finesse. That's why I stressed the word 'look.' Don't put it in words or strip *any* of their Committee posts. Just let the media do the work for you, following your subtle hints. The media's airing of these themes will provoke coarse, extremist comments from the Turks. Meanwhile, Reginald, you maintain your dignity, your impeccable bearing, your sartorial splendor, and polite demeanor. You will seem above the fray as they destroy themselves."

Regina displayed observable delight at these splendid, savvy suggestions, and she knew Reginald was similarly overcome.

Senator Clearwater wasn't far behind in his own delight. "I heartily concur with this strategy. And may I add that Ms. Melosay is one smart and compassionate lady, Mr. Speaker, to give you such advice when she is the leader of your opposition who would like to replace you some day as Speaker. There is a new kind of political patriotism emerging here."

The Speaker, signaling agreement with Clearwater, but directly addressing the Minority Leader, said, "Well, I really appreciate your words, Marcy. What they point to is a temporary 'Let's wait and see' posture on our part, along with my dropping of pregnant hints to the media about the shortcomings of the Turks. We also know that we must stay in close, confidential touch, OK?"

Speaking nearly at the same time, and with the same enthusiasm, Melosay and Senator Clearwater readily agreed. Regina stood up and asked, "How about some pasta with my special tomato sauce recipe, before you go?" The trio all gave a smiling, relieved, affirmative nod. It is always easier to decide not to have to make hard decisions.

The Movement Keeps on Snowballing

While this meeting was taking place and long into the night afterward, the Reporter was burning the midnight oil, deep in reams of data. The reason why even his associates call him the Reporter, rather than using his name, is because of his penchant not just for reviewing seemingly non-relevant databases but being able to put together information from these sources in unique, fresh reports.

At this all-nighter, he had come up with three new polls that showed a sharp increase in the number of eligible voters who knew the names of their members of Congress. Another item he linked to this finding was that, as he found when scrutinizing pictures of the marches and parades that came over his computer screen, the protesters were increasingly carrying signs picturing the faces of senators and congresspersons: a grim portrait, name, and date of birth, as if they were mug shots on the police blotter. Only the word "Wanted" was absent. In addition, he counted many primary challengers parading along with the marchers, joining as participants. They were not featured as leaders or given any other recognition, but the Reporter recognized them as he had studied their pictures earlier. The intrepid newspaperman blended all these separate findings into a story. His editor found this telling headline for the piece: "Loaded for Bear: The People Know Who They're Coming For."

The Summons Group Caucuses

What Doug Colebrook came to call "The Small Community" (after that seventy-five-year-old book by Arthur Morgan extolling how little groups have a unique ability to spur change), started flying into O'Hare Airport for their initial person-to-person strategy gathering. The billionaire reserved four floors of a large hotel and separate conference facilities. Obviously, privacy was a priority. Doug, who was planning to set the agenda, was well prepared to have them focus on one objective: Answering the questions of, first, what kind of changes, short- and long-term, must Congress make, given the historic groundswell heading its way, in order to refashion democracy? And, second: Who must be enlisted to move these well-conceived changes through Congress and over to the President with deliberate speed. Speed was of the essence as the more time passed, the more the public would begin to fatigue and the powerbrokers have a chance to mount a counterattack.

As Doug met many of the associates for the first time in person, he was reassured that his careful selection, based on what they did, said, and wrote, was valid. The people were very different from one another: anti-war veterans, shop stewards, engineers, farmers, social studies teachers, emergency medics, members of the repair trades, immigrant and native-born small business people, caregivers, street lawyers, factory supervisors, retired investment and economic specialists, physical therapists, sports coaches, and others. It wasn't that they were chosen for their experience or knowledge—though that was a positive—it was that Doug gauged them to have the right character and personality. He loved to read and was struck by the validity of what the ancient philosopher Heraclitus said: "Character is destiny." From his own study of life, Doug added his own aphorism: "Personality is decisive."

He did his homework on these arrivals the best he could, but he now found that some got through the screen—people he would not have chosen if he knew them better. They exhibited social justice concerns but were troubled personally. That's OK, he thought. Their presence will help etch the contrasts, highlighting the strengths of the majority.

For a three-day weekend, which was preceded by weeks of thought, they worked through the highest quality proposals, ones that had long been placed on the public table by the thinkers and doers of America. These included all areas concerning the establishment of a basic standard of living for everyone, the role of our country in the world—peace replacing war—and civic globalization as the measure of other interactions. In addition, the ideas of nurturing respect for global ecologies, the fostering of community, and the fulfillment of human possibilities, coupled with distinctive cultural tolerance, were deliberated.

The assemblage of people worked over these proposals so as to situate them in ways that made them more responsive to on-the-ground dynamics as well as to make them able to correct misperceptions that might arise. An expanded brain bank of specialists was put together for the time when they would be needed to contend with the obstruction of purported technicalities and procedures.

The participants also took turns relating the tumult in their regions and all agreed that speed was critical to press forward at each inflection point in order to keep the offensive momentum going and to deny the establishment any time to regroup and defeat the progressives' aims. One coach put it well: "We're here to plan for the end game, or at least the fourth quarter. All those good people who get us there deserve decisive reinforcements. And we must also remember to watch the terrain of the playing field as the nature of the game changes when we move from the streets to the suites."

"No, no, no," responded a sun-burnt farmer from New England. "I object to your last few words, 'the game changes when we move from the streets to the suites.' I'm from the land of town meeting forms of local government, and that's where that distinction you are making is not very apropos. Where I hail from, *we* are the legislature, taking over if our town selectmen do not do what we want. If that town meeting level doesn't work, we go to referendum. Our practice is about as close to having the streets *being* the suites as you can imagine. As I see it, taking our fight to the Congressional level is just a matter of scale, a difference in degree, not in kind. We must think about the coming weeks in that way or the big boys will make sure that the chasm between the streets and the gated suites becomes unbridgeable."

For Doug, the farmer's words were like a flash of brilliant light, a bolt from the blue that showed the necessary way to a seamless path to victory. It answered in a significant way the questions before this congregation that would emerge more fully as their movement went ahead. They didn't yet have all the details but they had a strategy.

On the last day, each participant chose his/her assignments to return home to their Congressional District. Each would be acting so as to increase their quality numbers (but still keeping the core to the size of small community) and to move with the much larger numbers of engaged residents who are getting the country, in baseball language, toward third base.

The Reporter Follows the Rat Trail

The Reporter cursed himself for not being in on the O'Hare meeting. He found out about it way too late to make it out to Chicago, being clued in at midnight via text just as he was going down to see how the night-shift exterminators were doing.

The workers were having a tougher time than they had anticipated. They told the Reporter that they were working under strict orders not to over-apply the chemicals since the Congress would be coming back as quickly as possible, leaving little time to air out the place. Having got rid of the cats, which, after being satiated with tasty rats, had turned into a self-indulgent nuisance, the managers discovered that the rats were not going quietly to their extermination. They were learning how to withdraw by day when most of the exterminators were prowling around, and to race around by night to forage.

Moreover, in another adaptive strategy, acting like trapped rats (or at least very harried ones), the rodents found their ways into areas of the Congress upon which no four-leg had ever trod. These spaces included bookcases, sofas, liquor cupboards, closets, and all kinds of secret enclaves that senior lawmakers used as privileged sanctuaries. The exterminators were instructed to be very careful not to become bulls-in-the-china closets on entering such sacred space. So, having to be extra careful meant the job took more time.

But progress was being made. As the Reporter learned, the nightly body count of slaughtered rats kept rising, then plateaued, which meant that with a little luck the dead-rat catch would start to decline because there were fewer rats left to deep six.

Ordinary reporters were satisfied to learn the chemicals used were called "rat point." The Reporter wanted to know the trade and scientific names of all the chemicals, which he checked out on the EPA and other databases. That tedious labor produced a significant exposé headlined: "Exterminators Using Chemicals Deployed in Vietnam and Iraq Wars."

As the Reporter noted, some of these chemicals were not licensed to be used on civilian sites, not to mention in the hallowed halls of Congress.

The rest of the media ran with the Reporter's initial scoop, adding many more interviews of dissenting experts condemning these chemicals and demanding a response from the pertinent federal regulatory agencies. By the time the furor subsided with the withdrawal of the offending chemicals, the work had been shut down for five days. The rats had a reprieve which they took advantage of by recovering lost ground.

Rat Revelry, Exterminators' Finishing Touches, and the People's Wrath

Somehow, by sheer randomness, the rats celebrated this temporary respite by an orgy in the Speaker's private bathroom, relieving themselves everywhere. Meanwhile, to replenish their ranks, pregnant mother rats kept giving birth to litter after litter deep in remote dark places.

The eradication period was now nearing a full month. For the homeless legislators, this was an intolerable delay, especially with some of the citizenry challenging why the legislators were continuing to receive their paychecks. They were loudly asserting that nothing in the law provided for "paid rat leave." In reaction to this, by remote, a near unanimous and frightened Congress passed a resolution naming March 31st as the last day for the exterminators. The workers were told that if they meet that deadline, they would get a fifteen percent bonus on their contracts.

Sure enough, money talks in the rat death business too. The extermination teams declared victory, on time, with the dead rat countdown to under fifty—a normal level—and prepared to evacuate the sprawling premises after a modest "job well done" ceremony proudly conducted by their trade association: The Unbreakable Fraternity of Rat Removers. As you can see, the fraternity had a keen sense of public relations.

But the American people had another ceremony in mind for that same evening. They sought to keep in the public eye the galvanizing symbolism of rats taking over Congress, especially at the very moment when the solons were attempting to re-establish BS politics-as-usual. Activists felt they needed the rats around until the people arrived to establish their own sovereignty. The rats were, so to speak, irreplaceable "place holders."

The first act of these public-spirited citizens was to clamber up to the roof of the Teamster's building, which enabled them to project a giant rat on the nearby Capitol Dome—a rat showing its teeth as if it was about to devour that building. The media photographers then sent the picture all over the country for millions to view on TV, their computer screens, smartphones, and in newspapers. Another raft of satiric and crude commentary ensued. The cartoonists and the widely syndicated *Doomsbury* had a field day, giving the electronic rat many anthropomorphic views and intents.

A second maneuver that took some attention away from the rat fraternity's pending celebration was the arrival of two eighteen-wheelers containing dainty little cages with a pet mouse for each member of Congress. On the cage was a picture of each lawmaker with the caption: "A pet mouse for your house" and, in small print, "Certified by Mice For Medical Research Labs, Inc." The team accompanying the trucks, which went to the rear of the Rayburn Office Building's loading dock, negotiated a deal whereby, in return for the trucks "going away," the exterminators would deliver each mouse cage to the reception desk of each member of Congress. It was done efficiently and quickly enough so that the eighteen-wheelers were gone before the commencement of the ceremony.

An Old Rat Sounds Off

The next morning in the *Washington Toast* there appeared a column by the newspaper's famous humorist Lean Beergarten titled, "From

Invasion to Extermination—the View from a Great, Great, Great Granddaddy Rat." The story went:

I am an old rat and have seen just about everything in my travels; gotten into many fights with rats, which I didn't start, and have the scars and wounds to prove it. Probably sired three thousand little rats from dozens of mothers. That's what male rats do: they eat, fight competitors, and hump lady rats. It's a good life and we as a species have survived everything humans have thrown at us: poisons, chemicals, mashing machines, drownings, sudden suffocating confinements with no exits, feral cats, hungry dogs, even snakes that can get into our crevices and nests. Once I just got away—though my then-family didn't—from sonic raticide—a high pitch blast that drove us mad. You sure have the killing tools. And, of course, your medical scientists vivisection us and our little mice relatives to death by the millions every year.

But in my long life I've never seen humans behave so stupidly as they have in this Congressional war against our frolics through their offices. Why stupid? Because it was an invasion of their own making. First, the casual scattering of much food and the conditions in the catacombs brought us into your domain. Then, the bringing in of the cats disrupted our normal, cautious comings and goings through our escape routes. What did you expect us to do?

Think about it. We're the ultimate survivors of the fittest, battling our way through life's dangers—unlike Congressional big shots, who rig their long careers so that they have little competition to contend with. And lack of competition stalls evolution of their species.

The whole ridiculous scene could have been prevented if humans were intelligent enough to apply Russian scientist Pavlov's approach, what's called "conditioned response." You could have stopped distributing crumbs and food wrappers all over the grounds. If we found nothing to eat after a few forays, we would have learned not to disturb your "nests."

Instead the Congress overreacted, paid for our annihilation, poisoned their own nests and corridors—you humans call it "blowback"—and provoked a people's rebellion that at this point knows no limits. In fact, for us, this uprising is an added plus. As more people come to town and march around and camp out, they tend to eat out and scatter food and packaging everywhere, giving us free provisions so that we can thrive and multiply. Just as often happens with your blundering militaristic overkill policies abroad, what has happened is that you've done it *to yourselves*.

However, our centuries of studying humans mean that your shortsighted actions are no surprise. Our sages tell us that rat lives are all about sacrifices. We're used to a culture of suffering and death. That's why we're so tough.

As our philosophers also remark, you humans, especially lawmakers, are the opposite. You're bullies until you're put into a corner, then you become criers, whiners, and whimperers. Combine that with the tendency of your plans to backfire and I can see the future. You think you've driven us from your premises. Let's say you have returned us to a normal level of what you sneeringly call "infestation." But now, due to your own increasingly noticed shortcomings, you may soon be evacuated by the very people who sent you here. Then we'll really hear some crybaby bawling.

We rats have never been much concerned with human history, though, as our rat chroniclers tell us, we've often had a paw in shaping it. We've had a big influence in the past as when our fleas took out nearly half of you in Europe during the 14th century "bubonic plague." I can't credit that all to our and the fleas' ingenuity. It was really due, again, to the stupidity of your rulers and clerics, who assassinated almost all the cats: our eternal enemies.

But the historical role you've given us now is different. During the plague years, we were death-dealing, but in this instance our influence may be life-liberating for millions of human beings, who may be freed from the yoke of your Congress and the marauding corporations that call its tune. You've outsmarted yourselves. Shall I say thinking you were too smart

Ralph Nader

for the rats, you ended up out of your comfort zone. All ratdom
nearby will be watching what happens next as we never seem
to get tired of viewing the heights and depths of human folly.
Survivingly yours,
A Very Old Rat

Young Turks Take the Offensive, Meeting Captains of Industry

Even if the Young Turks read Beergarten's animal fantasy, and probably they did not, not one of them would have creased a smile or been
prompted to snicker. They were perennially angry, self-righteous characters, always preaching to the persuaded, wrapping religion around
their promotion of "free market" greed, and seemingly devoid of any
sense of secular community. They were also quite fact-deprived, relying
on slogans, their chosen authority figures, and the elections they had
just won handily, brazenly not even hiding their agenda, which catered
to the desires of the rich and powerful or, as they called them, "the
Job-Creators." It was the latter "legitimacy," their skewed sense that the
people voted for that corporate welfare agenda (which was packaged as
a way to provide jobs and economic benefits to all), which fortified their
determination to tip the balance of power held by (the now ideologically questionable) Speaker in their favor on bill after bill, on budget
after budget.

What had the whole country up in arms—the invasion of the rats;
the widespread, vociferous reaction by the people, both left and right;
the hammering of Congress by the media—none of these contempo-
rary pressures bothered them at all. They still complacently looked back
on their easy last election, saw in the present, that the wobbly, now
repulsively leftish turncoat of the Speaker would have few deep-wal-
leted allies, and visualized that even if everything went wrong and they
lost their next election, a million-dollar-a-year position awaited them in

the offices of the plutocracy they had so vigorously served. How could anything or anybody, even their plummeting public approval ratings, change their minds?

Rather than reflect on the public's rejections of their type of politics, they would act, doing the exact thing the public was condemning them for, except in a bigger way. The Turks decided to go to New York for a frank meeting with the Chairman and his core cohort to tell them what they wanted to do, get their advice, and receive their tangible support, the latter meaning money, endorsements from the fawning business press. and access to the high-rollers' Rolodexes.

The meeting took place around the same gigantic conference table in New York, but with only a select part of the original cohort that had concluded by taking a "Let's wait and see" attitude. The remaining chairs were occupied by most of the "Young Turks" who made the trip up to what they believed was the real seat of the government—Wall Street.

The Chairman was happy to see them, opening the get-together with: "Welcome to all of you whose sterling voting records speak to your being our staunchest allies, except that, if you will permit me to say, none of us appreciate your recent bandying about of that awful phrase 'crony capitalism.' I realize this is just your way of playing to the public, and you don't intend to have anything you say about these business buccaneers reflected in legislation, but I also think you should understand that the so-called 'excesses' of 'crony capitalism' is just our effort to take back what was taken from us in the first place by the thinly veiled socialists down there in Washington.

"Forgive me. I just had to get that off my chest. In any event, I don't want to get into this argument with you. There's more urgent business that I gather you wish to run by us."

A Young Turk, well turned out in one of Armani's finest, spoke first. "Mr. Chairman, let us get right to the point—and thank you, by the way, for having us here. None of what is bursting out around the country frightens us. We've seen these summer squalls come and go before. As they say, the only poll that counts is on Election Day and a glance backward shows that was a sweeping victory for our party, even with all the pro-corporation bills, which some rabble rousers are now questioning, we got through the House on the open public record. So there was no deceptive advertising that our adversaries so often accuse us of buying. What the public saw, they must have liked as they gave us a thumping success. And, by the way, Alf Radar and all the other nut-jobs running for independent tickets were laughed out of the race.

"We're not here to worry about this momentary outcry against us, but we are here today because we want to replace the Speaker and his cronies, who can't seem to get with the program. If there was any doubt about the need to do this, his appearance on Mr. Toad's *Meet the Press* should have convinced any timorous doubters on our side. I presume you saw his conversion on live television and hopefully it was before you had your breakfast. Otherwise you would have downloaded what you ate into the sink after hearing his disgusting remarks."

Since the first meeting, a number of foreign members had joined the business leaders group. Now one, with streaked gray/black hair and a high-end Wolfgang Joop suit, joined the conversation. "I'm from Germany, but have been on the board of the New York Stock Exchange for ten years. May I ask just what you found so objectionable to what the Speaker said?"

This mild-mannered remark set off another of the Turks, this one well served by a pricey Hugo Boss suit. He laced out, "Mr. Chairman, are we to be judged by the twisted standards of this German fellow or by tried-and-true USA free market principles? Cutting the budget of our national defense, collecting more taxes, calling our environmental bills 'doubletalk' and the laws' titles hypocritical while actually having named several himself, and, adding insult to injury, slandering our revered Chairman of the House Rules Committee by calling him 'Chairman Nyet.' And then to top off this crazed interview, the Speaker talked about a Bastille moment if the Congress doesn't bend, predicting it would end up, otherwise, in the dustbins of history. Isn't that enough? And who knows what else he would have said to feed the appetites of our Marxist press had he had more time on the program."

The Chairman, making a gesture as if he were throwing a friendly arm on the Boss-clad Turk, tried to calm him: "I don't think you fellows in Washington are getting the big picture. Frankly, your views are just a little too parochial for any of our tastes here.

"What I mean is, from a broader perspective, there is nothing very revolutionary about what the Speaker said or on what or whom he based his opinions in discussing our hallowed past and present. We are in an expanding global economy and we have to keep abreast of what is going on in those nations that we defeated in World War II and left utterly destitute. Now, like phoenixes, they have risen from the ashes and become sharp global competitors.

"This is not to say that I don't also realize where you folks are coming from. You have philosophical convictions, not business strategies; you have donors who insist on your maintaining those convictions as a way to contrast with your political opposition; and you have core supporters, less savvy businesspeople, who have attached their fear to what they personally see as their heritage, their traditions, all things that may be taken away by a very rapidly changing world.

"Again, if you'd adopt a wider view, you'd correctly identify that the Main Street vs. Wall Street slogan is not just a neat, politically combative rallying cry. It is a recognition that the Wall Streeters are far more able to transfer their costs—of regulation, of paperwork, or of taxes—to others than can a small Main Street business. And, if that doesn't work, our attorneys can always take advantage of numerous waivers in rigid existing laws that are difficult and expensive for smaller businesses to use. But keep in mind, a huge percentage of what is called small business are franchisees who, I must admit, are entitled to greater support from the giant chain franchisors in order to level the playing-field a bit. The point being: this conflict is not simply ideological, though that's how you Washingtonians seem to interpret it, but involves dollars and cents issues."

Another slightly older Young Turk took the floor. Being more mature than the others, he favored a conservative herringbone suit by Tom Ford. He spoke in measured tones. "Mr. Chairman, what you've just said raises so many questions to digest that, if you don't mind, I would like to consult in private with my colleagues for a few minutes."

The Chairman, who was bending over backward to accommodate these (as he privately called them) "nincompoops," said, "No problem. Jeeves, will you please guide these good friends to Conference Room #4 down the hall?"

Young Turks Need to Reboot

Inside Conference Room #4, the Turks, who were much more non-plussed with their reception than they had let show on their faces when they were in the presence of the corporate bigwigs, were doing some quick reassessing.

The older Turk was quick to spell out what all his younger, less well-dressed colleagues, were sensing. "We have to face facts. The Chairman is really with the Speaker. Maybe the Speaker knew this before going on *Meet the Press*. We are in less of a comfortable position than we thought. Say what you will about our Main Street support, made up of many small business people, without Wall Street we are substantially isolated because Wall Street has so many hooks, so many controls over Main Street, they can work around us if they so wish.

"You'd think it would be enough that through their influence on the Federal Reserve, the big bankers get their way with interest rates, credit, and so much else. And, on top of that, Wall Street is the Empire of crony capitalism, meaning most of the goodies are reserved for the inner circle. You heard what the Chairman said about not wanting to get into an argument with us on crony capitalism. It is pretty hard for honest small businesses to compete with crony capitalism and a servile Congress. However, to return to my opening point, we can't frighten these moguls by saying we have Main Street at our backs. They have their ways of controlling Main Street and ousting us from our cozy relationship with the voters if they decide that it is in their interest."

One Turk, dressed in a blue Prada, hadn't been able to get in a word yet. He was a pragmatist who could turn on a dime. Having already digested the veiled rejection of their position by the moguls, he quickly went for a new tack. "It looks grim. We can't afford a blow up, a heated argument, when we get back to the Chairman and his buddies. My instinct tells me that we should soft pedal our views here and concentrate our fire on undermining Speaker Blamer in Congress where we'll be on our own turf. The Speaker cannot get much through if the House Rules Committee Chair doesn't allow the bill to come up for a vote, hardly an unusual practice for the House leader that the Speaker has labeled Chairman Nyet!"

Another hot-headed member of their group, clad in Dolce & Gabbana, was thinking even further ahead. He put it like this: "What if the Speaker is no longer the Speaker. What if he just goes poof? Can't we put together a majority of the GOP caucus to oust him? Or, do you'all think his control's too enduring, too deep, and too connected for that to happen?" The Dolce wearer was a southerner.

Many liked what they heard, and murmured affirmatively as they considered this route.

Of all of them, the next Young Turk to speak, kept his mind most focused on their present situation. After all, they had come here to talk with these moneybags, not argue about legislative strategy. He brought his fellow lawmakers back to the present. "I think we all heard enough from the Chairman to grasp that we're not going to get what we came for.

"I say we face it, and move on. We need to let these rich guys know that they *need us*. Don't they get it? We're like a dike standing between them and the public. It's us who muscled through the Trade Agreement's Fast Track, who starve corporate crime enforcement budgets, who keep the capital gains and dividend tax rate lower than the regular income tax, who preserve the 'carried interest' charade for the hedge funds, who stopped a Wall Street transaction tax from being imposed, and oppose any breakup of the big banks which, we claim, are too big to fail. Just about ninety percent of the people want that last one.

"That ought to be a long enough laundry list of good turns and giveaways that we have delivered to make them realize how valuable we are. From our side, I bid you to remember we need to keep our lines open to *them* and retain their financial support for our campaigns. So let's do nothing more to antagonize them. I really believe they don't want a division to occur that forces them to have to choose between us and the Speaker's much larger camp. In short, let's cool it and show that they need us. We'll have our say, have a drink, and leave on good terms."

And that is just what happened to the mutual relief of all concerned, at least on the surface. As the Tom Ford dresser remarked on the trip back to Washington, "When you don't have the cards, don't try to force the play."

Dissident Billionaires Get Into the Act

At about the same time that this was transpiring in New York City, three multi-billionaires gathered at the Washington, DC, home of one of them—a happy-go-lucky fellow who always seemed to be at the right place at the right time as an early investor. Most of the start-ups which he put money into turned out to be blockbusters. Maybe it was intuition, but he made it big by pouring money into several small Internet firms just before their shares went through the roof.

As part of his strategy for finding promising ventures, he felt he had to have wide knowledge, not only of the business climate but of the general social environment. He spent lots of time reading, looking at documentaries, and knowing a lot about what's going on in the enveloping worlds of politics, business, and popular culture.

The second very rich person, who was from the West Coast, called himself a progressive libertarian. This meant he didn't take libertarianism, the freedom to do what you will, so far that it boomerangs, hurting yourself and other people.

His views made a splash recently when he revealed them in a lengthy article he wrote for *Politico* arguing for a fifteen-dollar an hour minimum wage as being good for everyone, from the bottom all the way up to those like himself perched near the top of the economic pyramid. What caught the Big Boys' attention in their executive suites was his remark: "While pundits look into their crystal ball and worry about interest rates going up, inflation coming, or more job-displacing automation if this minimum wage increase is instituted, what I see, if it is not instituted, are pitchforks."

"Pitchforks!" cried one famous boss scooping lobster meat from the shells with one of those little forks as he sat in a well-appointed millionaires' club.

The third super-affluent one inherited and invested so well that he could devote himself to his two other great loves: board games and free soup. He divided his time between playing advanced chess in Chicago and responding to hundreds of soup kitchen appeals so as to pay for ten-million nutritious meals a year around the country.

All three men, who knew each other from their years at Princeton, had watched closely the Congressional rat invasion and the exploding public reaction, including all its nuances. That's why they got together just about the time the Congress was reconvening with the successful and expensive—one hundred million dollars—completion of the Extermination Program. The billionaires got to chatting on the phone about developments and decided it would be worthwhile to have a meeting.

Over mint juleps, they started talking. Happy Go led off, mincing no words and putting all his cards and thoughts on the table. "You know, all this hustle and bustle around the country—really very impressive and creative and deeply felt—seems to be without an organizational form. No one is harnessing this political energy busting out. I know enough about street movements—it's one of the things I've kept tabs on over the years—to comprehend that people's energy unharnessed and without full-time organizers helping to shape it, can peter out, even if it doesn't encounter formidable police and other opposition. I suggest we appoint ourselves funders of the harnessing stage, helping to bankroll the movement straight through the working out of viable agendas to their enactment by our sweetly shaken Capitol Hill."

Our libertarian was pleasantly shocked, because he had come prepared to propose the same game plan. "Perfecto, Happy! Just what I had on my mind.

"Let's not complicate what needs to be done. It's been in the air a long time and now it's finally coming into view. The trains are on the track. They are being refueled by the hour. The destination is known. The product delivered is overdue justice for the people."

He had a laptop open in front of him and now he turned it so his friends could see the colorful rats on parade, driving out tuxedoed legislators. "Just look at those compelling posters."

He set aside his computer and spoke earnestly. "Here's my take. Let's make the changes, the faster the better. Momentum is not only for competitive sports. Moreover, some of the tactics we hit them with have to be ones that the politicians have *not* had to confront before. The unknown breeds indecision, conflict over how to respond, delays, recriminations. Happily, as you know from your study of history, such inept reactions to the unexpected are themselves beautifully predictable. Look how a battalion of black rats paralyzed them. Those guys from Vancouver who put out the magazine *Badbusters* sense this, as evidenced by their comment on the rodent revolution where they push for 'culture-jamming,' the disruption of media images and messages. But the pressure has to be polite, urgent, relentless and *in personam*, to use the legal term. That is, each media disruption has to be laser-targeted directly at one single legislator and his or her immediate circle of handlers, advisors, and mentors. But always first and last on the singular lawmaker. That will get maximum results."

The chess-playing billionaire also felt they were all of the same mind. Of course, this had already been established in their numerous phone conversations, but it made more impact when they conversed face to face. He opened his heart to his friends. "I like what both of you are saying. You know, from my previous conversations, about the Summons Group that Doug Colebrook is stitching together very tightly out of Chicago. I've recently been helping him with some expenses to fly his network to a meeting. His focus is exactly *in personam* and the summons-from-the-voters' idea is the personal carrier of agendas right back to the Congress. Zoom, zoom, dead on target, no zigzag!

"As I see it, the Summons Group wants an understandable, unified agenda setting out items that repeated opinion polls show already have majoritarian support. The agenda items are not talking points, but rather carefully drafted legislation vetted by leading experts in law and other fields. Having the demands in this finished form not only reduces the risk of continual bickering, but meshes well with the essential approach that our libertarian friend outlined, which was 'the faster the better' as far as being the way to increase the likelihood of enactment. If the Summons people keep up a quick tempo, the powerful, corporate members of the political and business elite, so used to being on top and getting their way, will have no time to mount an effective opposition. Sure, they will have time for mass propaganda, but no time to engage in their historic practice of dividing and ruling. That's why I just love your 'pitchforks' metaphor in that it evokes the image of resolute unity, each prong being a different focused group, all linked together at the base."

"Well," began Happy, "what you have told us about the Summons group has brought me to look into and reflect upon one aspect of social movements that has sometimes been an Achilles heel for them: leadership. Harnessing the energy has generally involved leaders, mostly meritorious leaders or charismatic leaders.

"But at this point in the trajectory of the rat-inspired uprising, I sense that selecting leaders will create dissension, delay, and vulnerability to expected opposition strategies. You know the saying, 'You go up with leaders and you go down with leaders.' In other word, if a leader is discredited or is corrupt, it can take down the movements.

"I know you guys sometimes rib me for all the time I spend with my head stuck in history books, but, to go to my favorite source for relevant examples, let me recall some things about the American Revolution against Great Britain. Many of those social movement pioneers made the distinction in organizations between leaders (top down stuff) and leaderships (people who know how to get things done in their area of competence). I like the style adopted by the farmers in Massachusetts in 1774. No pronounced leaders. Just rotating leadership tasks. They combined that with clear goals and the use of pivotal locations as they confronted the Tory stooges of King George III who were trying to enforce the monarch's commands.

"To forestall your objections, because I think you might say, with truth, that we're in a far more complex society, I would underline that, no matter the different circumstances, human personalities, characters, and the steady virtues, frailties, and vices are still the same. Otherwise, why do people today still flock to Shakespearean plays and ancient Greek theater?

"Here," he went on, facing his laptop in their direction, "I taped a sequence on We-Span TV, which illustrates how the new people in the struggle are handling the leadership dilemma." Happy had archived an interview by the well-known host Ryan Mutton, sporting his trademark muttonchops, of the early-bird activists who had already arrived in Washington, DC, to keep pressing for the reforms the rat invasion had gotten people to think about.

"Who's your leader?" asked Mutton. The three viewers knew that the corporate news media had to have a leader to fix upon whenever there was any kind of demand for change.

Ralph Nader

Almost as if she had been reading the same books as Happy, the first person to speak said, "Everyone is a leader for whatever job needs to be done."

A couple of others chimed in, "We speak for ourselves," almost talking over each other, laughing at the confusion.

Mutton didn't lose any of his aplomb and went on blandly, "OK, then I'll ask some questions and any of you can answer. Whoever sees it as his/her job."

Happy switched off the television, over his chess-playing friend's objections. "Hey, I was getting into that."

Happy grinned—nothing fazed him—and said, "I'll send you the whole tape. Right now, I want to segue to a related point. When the agendas have to be conveyed to Congress to enact, a number of spokes-people will have to stand forth as representatives of the whole. What I want to emphasize to the movement people is that they have to hold tight reins on the people's spokespeople as they engage with the leg-islative branch. That is why the very natures of the mandates must be unique. They must know they are not there to seek compromises and negotiated, watered-down settlements. These spokespeople are coming with completely drafted legislation, driven by irresistible rhetoric rooted in irrebuttable evidence, filed by so many members of both parties as to approach unanimity: a consensus that totally overrides the insidious procedural traps that have marked the Hill's culture and the reign of Chairman Nyet."

The libertarian, always concerned with what role he could play, as opposed to worrying about what others were doing, struck in, "Let's back up a bit. How are we going to fuel this emerging wonder of Amer-ican history? What I'm thinking is that we should have in our minds a minimum of money, split three ways, that can be drawn down expe-ditiously and accountably. In that way, we will not be bothered to pay expenses pouring in, coming in dribs and drabs. That could test our tolerances.

"I suggest two hundred and fifty million dollars each and, if things are going swimmingly in the next few weeks before the competitive pri-maries start, we can quietly agree to add more. Remember Ben Franklin saying to a woman outside that small Philadelphia building in 1787 on the completion of the draft of the Constitution (though without yet the

Bill of Rights), when she asked, 'What have you made, Mr. Franklin?' He replied, 'A Republic if you can keep it.'"

He nodded to Happy. "I threw that in to show you that you're not the only one who has spent many a night with a history book in one hand and a notebook in the other.

"Let me return to Franklin's thought, and build on it, perhaps a bit melodramatically. Perhaps if someone were to ask us what we were doing, we might say: We're keeping a failing ship of state from capsizing so we can bring it to a new and long-dreamed-of destination."

And, recalling the speaker's noteworthy pitchfork reference in his essay, the chess player said, "We are all ready to *pitch* in."

While Happy, having his mind on the libertarian's apropos reference to old Franklin, added, "I'm ready right now to *fork* over the Benjamins."

Whereupon they began taking assignments to assure that the most efficacious and sober modes of this democracy-rising renaissance could focus on its goals without constantly worrying about the bills.

A Pay-For-Play Congress on the Ropes

Still favoring the ostrich option, once the cleaners' ceremony was over, the chambers properly fumigated and the new rules about not leaving crumbs around the suites were in place, the lawmakers spent very little time ruminating about the rat invasion which, if it was up to them, would be erased from the national memory as thoroughly as the rats seem to have been from the buildings' pipes.

Reporters who reminded them of what had just passed were told either "What's past is past" or "That's ancient history."

This reaction wasn't a manifestation of post-traumatic stress, but rather a hidden avowal that they were suffering *current*-traumatic stress in the form of a swarm of candidates challenging them in the primaries. Little else mattered, though they, of course, didn't say this publically. Almost panicked, they ramped up their clamoring for campaign cash,

Ralph Nader

carried out particularly in icky meetings with Political Action Committees (PACs) in restaurants and hotel suites in Washington.

They universally thought of them as "icky," because, accomplished as some of the lawmakers were in this practiced kabuki dance, which took place on the line between legalized bribery and shakedown, no one relished playing the role of asking for cash for promises or financial rewards for past legislative sales.

Seasoned analyst Ron McFain put it succinctly during the Republican presidential primary in New Hampshire back in 2000. He described, "a campaign finance system [that was] nothing less than an elaborate peddling scheme in which both parties conspire to stay in office by selling the country to the highest bidder." But few put it more succinctly and blatantly than Pennsylvania Republican Senator Boies Pemrose. Over a century ago, he explained to a gathering of his business supporters, "I believe in a division of labor. You send us to Congress; we pass laws under . . . which you make money . . . and out of your profits you further contribute to our campaign funds to send us back again to pass more laws to enable you to make more money."

Odorous as this ritualized auction is to all lawmakers—for it's annoying and degrading to put oneself up like a Victorian lampshade to be bought by the highest bidder—they constantly decline to act together to put an end to it. The repeatedly announced pathetic excuse by those who at least have the courage to even allude to the matter, "I will not unilaterally disarm before my opponents." Not the most cogent response in that reform would come if the lawmakers all dropped their ties to their cash providers at the same time.

It was this refusal to act on the impulses of their inner woman or man in the way Speaker Blamer had, that meant the stench of stasis grew worse from election cycle to election cycle. Plunging into this ignoble cash-register politics, the lawmakers incurred even more denunciations. Even the usually indifferent-to-elite-wrongdoing mass media reported the campaign contributions of the moneybags, and fuller public reporting of it was easily accessible on websites for those interested. And for a public fed up with the antics of what more people were calling the "Senatorial Rat Riders" or the "Representative Rat Fleers," new reports and rumors of the payola-seeking taking place as the legislators returned to business-as-usual mode started a whole new round of public attack and ridicule.

Ironically enough, while the current lawmakers were begging for more contributions, almost licking the shoes of the well-heeled, in order to help them overcome their newly appearing opponents, the primary challengers rode on this wave of revulsion against this pay-for-play culture, and punctuated it mercilessly during their speeches and debates with the incumbents. To say that the polls were dropping, like thermometers during a sudden freeze, for the Congress as a whole and, unusually, even for individual members in home district polls of their constituents, is to understate what was really a plummet, like the drop of a roller coaster, going south in most cities, to single digits. The people wanted them, OUT, OUT, OUT.

The challengers weren't the only ones holding get-togethers to denounce the ongoing corruption. The people's movement was meeting publically constantly. The first of daily rallies—growing larger each day—took place in front of the expansive back lawn of the US Capitol. The message was devastating in its simplicity. The demands were specific on the placards and banners. But more broad-gauged was the human-voiced call out, over and over again, enhanced by the hypnotic, low drum beat, the same used by the ancient Roman Army on the march: BOOM, BOOM, slowly; BOOM, BOOM, BOOM, BOOM quickly. This underlay the call out of: "RESIGN, RESIGN [slowly, then], RESIGN, RESIGN, RESIGN, RESIGN [quickly], ALL OF YOU. YOU ARE COLLECTIVELY GUILTY OF HIGH CRIMES AND INJUS-TICES. WE THE PEOPLE GAVE YOU THE AUTHORITY AND THEN WE GAVE YOU THE POWER OF ELECTIVE OFFICE. YOU TURNED THAT POWER AGAINST US. WE WANT IT BACK. WE WANT IT BACK. RESIGN, RESIGN ... RESIGN, RESIGN, RESIGN, RESIGN!"

Something of a mouthful, but repeated and repeated, it became a mantra that strengthened resolve and focused purpose.

Seeing this on TV, agreeing with every word and wanting to be part of it, by car, train, bus, and airplane, the people started coming to join the daily call-out before Congress. Once there, they found other tasks to accomplish along with chanting, as different manifestations of the democracy surge began to take shape.

Ralph Nader

Summoned to Washington

Doug Colebrook and his cooperators decided it was time to expand operations to Washington, DC. The preliminary work and agendas were ripe for a deeper engagement, which would swing into the *in personam* focus which the Summons group's presence in the nation's capital would facilitate.

The adequate funding, which was given at just the right time by the billionaire trio, relieved the group of restraints and restrictions that were dollar-based. The fact that they chose not to work in the media spotlight was extremely useful in keeping them away from distractions so they could sort out the talents, tasks, and coordinations of this band of brothers and sisters. They knew that the tranquility would soon end, as they entered the fray more directly, and they were preparing for a transition that would be shaped by them. As they conceived it, moving to Washington was but an extension of the steadfast summons-driven activity being carried on back in the districts. The circuits had been carefully organized back home so that the plug, once put in the socket in Washington, could flow with energy, lighting up the arena where Congressional voting takes place.

The Cooperators, as they now called themselves, arrived ready to initiate an ingenious approach. They would tap into the expertise of the appropriate think tanks and citizen groups, but steer clear of the occupational hazards of these organizations, which included bickering, intrigue, and purported, overblown claims of influence on their members around the country.

To accomplish their purposes, the Cooperators located advocates for very well-thought-out legislation for reforming the campaign finance system, for progressive taxation that would give the country needed revenues to fund progressive policy goals, for providing facilities that enable focused organized civic cooperation associations where people would have the space to voluntarily band together to redress imbalances of power and foster community self-reliance.

Besides drawing from the think tanks and already organized citizen groups, the Cooperators knew they could get help from those who had impressive expertise, however subdued, among retired dissenting, military, security, and diplomatic persons. These experienced Americans could inform them regarding military/security budgets as well as on foreign policies that prevent wars and enhance standards of living, health, and safety. Once in Washington they soon learned of other groups that had developed budgets that represented the values of justice and compassion with attention to workers, children, and posterity. They found seasoned, articulate promoters of energy conversions away from fossils and nuclear and toward renewables. The Cooperators had hardly anticipated that so much data-driven common sense and experience would so quickly flow into their modest offices. As Doug Colebrook remarked eloquently, "The traditional virtues have a way of simplifying the common good. Invidious motivations complicate to hide. They build in cancers against public interest; twist, turn, obfuscate, and commercialize in order to subordinate civic values to short-term commercialism."

The Cooperators didn't have to prove themselves to gain entry to the varied progressive organization they found in Washington. They drew on their support back home to earn the respect of these organizations and readily accepted cross-monitoring and checking of their submissions by other specialists. The spreading impression that the Cooperators had large financial resources at their beck and call did not harm the alacrity with which their calls were returned.

They learned that many of the honest experts tapped by them were frustrated, daunted, and discouraged after witnessing years of the crude monetization of the nation's public institutions. But their spreading sadness had not dented their work ethic, because they remained committed to the belief that someday the situation would change so they had better be ready. Their files were gold mines. The Cooperators were enthused to discover in the archives scores of enlightened bills filed over the past century by senators and representatives of both parties but never passed, sometimes never even heard, but kept as a record of what our country could become. Publicizing and taking inspiration from these bills showed that the Cooperators were moving with the rhythms of the best of the past as formulated by legislators of conscience from all parts of the country, and this strengthened the standing of the Cooperators' missions.

Ralph Nader

Other citizen groups provided the Cooperators with excellent comparative material showing that in Western countries from Australia and New Zealand and Canada to Western Europe, for a long time people had enjoyed the fruits of social justice movements and multi-party vigor, giving them more vibrant polities and more citizen rights, although recently the virus of corporate financial globalization was destabilizing their political economies and fraying the edges of their productive and distributional practices. These materials provided quite a lesson for the public, showing that people in nations not aggregatedly wealthier than ours have obtained higher wages, stronger unions, universal health care, good pensions, highly used modern public transit, one month or more of paid annual vacation, free university education, well-maintained parks, and support for the arts, paid maternity leave, daycare, family sick leave, and more humane criminal justice and prison policies. This fortified the Cooperators' position beyond their expectations, as they were astounded by the wealth of material.

As each new bit of information was gleaned, these studied "assets" were conveyed to the Cooperators' fast expanding constituencies and informal alliances, given out both person-to-person and over the Internet, even reaching the world of teenagers who were starting to understand the stakes they had in what was transpiring.

Doug and his civic kin particularly wanted expertise in simplification. While most experts are trained to dote on complexity, the ones the Cooperators were searching for would be able to simplify laws, regulations, forms, red tape and those uncompetitive sign-on-the-dotted-line fine print contracts. They also needed experts who could do *weeding*, ones who could pinpoint outdated, useless laws and laws that shoveled taxpayer monies into crony capitalism, all of which needed to be repealed. This expertise, more often than not, was available at self-described conservative think tanks and related civic organizations.

On this note, someone brought up at a left/right meeting, that the Canadian Medicare Bill, written in the 1960s, which provided full healthcare with free choice of doctors and physicians (i.e., public insurance and private delivery of health services) was all of thirteen pages long. By comparison, the new health insurance legislation in the US ran over fifteen hundred pages with thousands of pages of regulations. The abundance of confusing detail and bureaucraticized language confused and froze people in bewildering ways.

The Cooperators task force on this specific issue challenged the rule-writers, who were crafting a new health insurance law, to explain everything in plain English. For they saw that what those who had put together the current legislation couldn't explain was the enormous time expended over exemptions, waivers, co-payments, deductibles, and tax consequences that regular citizens were obliged to endure, suffer, or even be brought down by when they fell into innocent violations. The task force well knew that Canada covers all its people at half the average per capita cost of what in the US the wasteful, corrupt, incomprehensible billing industry manages to impose year after year on American citizens, not counting millions of people without insurance.

The Cooperators realized that while the hard-lined conservatives they worked with understood the corporate control problems, they pigheadedly insisted on free market solutions. They could not, however, provide any very convincing facts or results to testify to real-world cases where their honestly-held abstract philosophy, actually proved workable or beneficial, especially as they consistently overlooked the perverse incentives and exclusions that reined in the health insurance fee for service business, resulting in avoidable loss of life and other physical and psychological harm to consumers, workers, and other citizens.

In working with collaborators of all ideological stripes, the Cooperators tried always to determine and separate expertise from such things as fact-deprived ideology and biased or hidden agendas. Obviously their own preference was for democratic, open community action, when individuals were unable to cope with the forces arrayed against them or simply unable as individuals to acquire what they needed without engaging in common action. While this suggested an idealism in their preferences, at bottom, the Cooperators were very empirical. They wanted to leave open what scientists called "options for revision." This meant they constantly sought nourishment from their base. They backed a devolution of activities to local levels wherever possible to enrich and advance continual improvements into the future.

A New, Formidable Progressive
Alliance is Formed

With Congress back in session, the Reporter was back at his post. It did not take him very long to note a fervent mobilization of progressive, and sometimes libertarian/conservative lawmakers in both Houses. While other reporters were mesmerized by the right-wing revolt against the Speaker, the Reporter kept his eyes on a real political alignment in formation, being cemented without much ballyhoo, and calling itself the All American Caucus (AAC). This transpartisan alliance was not bipartisanship in the old sense. They were not meeting to cut the difference between them so as to locate themselves in the lukewarm middle. They met to see where there was, issue by issue, principled common ground for action. Where there was no agreement, the subject was dropped.

About one hundred and five representatives and senators joined AAC. Some were seasoned Congressional veterans; others made up for their short experience with hard work and a fresh optimism about making history. They lacked the hard-to-suppress hopelessness of the sensitive old-timers, whose faith in positive change had been dimmed by the erosion of years mired in gridlock.

The ACC's agenda was quite similar to that of the Cooperators and they promptly reached out to initiate a working relationship with them. Both groups knew that inside and outside pressures were critical to aid them in getting enacted legislation to the White House. Tactically, they decided to lay low and keep their alliance out of the news as they prepared a very solid groundwork of considerable intricacy, fitting their members for action, equipped with carefully written legislation, without having the press on their back and the fulminating talk shows baying at the moon.

One thing the alliance didn't figure on was the Reporter's unparalleled contacts. Tipped off by the adversaries of the AAC inside the hardcore Rules Committee, the Reporter wrote a fifteen-hundred-word scoop that named names, meetings, and even mentioned some upcoming moves. Given everything going on around the country and in Washington, DC, the scoop did not cause much surprise. It served to intensify the time-sensitivity of the AAC, which had one eye on the upcoming primaries as a widely recognized deadline for decisions, and the other eye on the rampant impatience of the rapidly multiplying, enraged public. As one of the Alliance's originators, Representative Christina Eckhardt, said, "The shortness of time is on our side."

Something else was on their side. Rats! Every day several rats were seen scurrying across the carpets of some Congressional offices, seemingly trying to escape the whole complex, but trapped in it by the closure of every aperture by the exterminators.

The CIA analysts called it one of their favorite words, "blowback." Exits had been sealed, food was no longer left lying around and so the rats were hungry, looking for any tiny bit of food and spot of water. And each time a rat emerged, the staff went crazy; some fled to their homes, others started weeping or got furious. "When will it ever end?" seemed to be their common cry. It didn't help calm things down when many witnessed a designated office rat hunter, left on site by the exterminator company, bludgeon a cornered rat to a messy death. Nor did it quiet the ravenous reporters looking for a daily rat story for the insatiable masses, who could never get enough of those rodents. For the AAC folks, the perennial rodent stories in the news did serve to maintain the public ridicule, the hooting and howling that seemed to have instigated the positive transformation of the dignity-obsessed Speaker of the House of Representatives along with promoting an expanding abandonment of public apathy

The People's Tide Flows In

Meanwhile, by car, bus, rail, plane and even by bicycles and by foot, people of all ages, backgrounds, and places continued to pour into Washington. They filled the restaurants and the motels. They usually had to find a room in a city where there were few affordable apartments but many large, under-inhabited houses whose longtime owners

Ralph Nader

wanted to make some money to pay for their property taxes and repairs. So they were renting to the new arrivals.

The ways these visitors made their voices heard were quite imaginative. There was a cavalcade of horseback riders in a procession down Constitution Avenue resplendent with the signs, "Pass this . . ." or "Pass that . . ." always ending with the ominous "*or Else.*" One horseman was using his trumpet to raise the emotional level of the demonstration, which was fully covered in the press. Others joined the daily "*resign . . . or else*" rally going on at the backside of the Capitol while mini-demonstrations were becoming daily events in front of the White House and at other major government buildings containing departments and agencies. Even those agencies in the suburbs, such as the Pentagon, the CIA, the Patent Office, or the Food and Drug Administration, where the employees had thought they would be beyond reach, did not escape the rallying.

As the arriving tenants began to converse with their hosts, they learned about the de facto "colony" of the District of Columbia. Very few visitors knew about DC's absence of voting rights for members of Congress. DC had a delegate who could watch but not vote. These first timers in the city also learned there was a push for DC statehood. Some became indignant and added this to the grievances that had drawn them to the city. They were riled up enough to make placards calling for the proposed state of Columbia, parading them in front of the White House.

Visiting Your Local Congressperson *In Situ*

Not surprisingly there were a lot of freelance, unaffiliated organizers among the popular inflow of citizens, and being self-starters, they took their own initiatives. One of them rented space near Congress from which emanated scores of people dropping in on their own member of Congress. The Congressional corridors, until then filled by grasping lobbyists, began to be utilized by common people with uncommon pursuits.

This store-front organizer was no mere dispatcher, though he did handle logistics for the visitors so that they could properly schedule their visits. The fellow once was a staffer for a state senator in Massachusetts, in charge of handling letters from constituents. He was familiar with the granular, easy-to-miss differences in the way letters were written, which determined what got attention and what went straight to the circular file. In the latter group were the "We protest; we demand" ones. The store-front guy offered free, thirty-minute-long orientation classes several times a day in which he explained how to compose these missives and also how to approach their district legislators, giving the benefit of his experience to the human flow in and out of his gathering rooms.

He advised visitors not to do all the talking but make their points and ask the lawmakers or their staff for their reactions orally and in writing for later reference. As Storefront explained, politicians love to have their visitors do the talking so that they can simply smile and make no commitments or judgments. He counseled the visitors to exude some mystery about how large their circle was and who was in it. He said they should have factual questions written that require the staff to get the answers from, for example, the Congressional Research Service. In the process of finding information, the staff would be learning about their concerns. Moreover, he said, in talking to one group, "Don't leave unless you give the staff and the legislator a clear impression that you and your group are only going to get stronger when you meet next time either here or back in their district or state. You may wish," he added, "to ask for a town meeting some weeks hence and inquire about how many names on a requesting petition he or she would like to see before coming to your community to talk about your chosen subject. Finally, do your homework on the politician's record and background before you show up."

The storefront fellow wagged his finger and said, with a trace of sadness, "Too many voters are in awe of the aura of power in the Congressional offices and just make nice. That means they leave empty-handed. Politicians know full well how to be very polite and empty. It's practically a job requirement."

Prepared with instructions on how to make the most of their stop-ins, the visitors piled up the meetings with their senators and representatives, who were often unnerved to find how different, how well prepared, how determined their constituents were by comparison with what they were used to. What they were asked about were often things the congresspeople would have preferred not to talk about, and when they left, the visitors impressed them to no end by saying such things as they were now on the way to meet with the lawmaker's primary opponents. The smooth, seldom-seen-through-public-relations veneer that coated Congressional offices like a fine varnish didn't begin to work with these people, whose attitude was simply, and (for the lawmakers) shockingly, "You work for us; we are the people calling for these necessities; you will do what we want . . . or else."

"Wow" and "Whew," both the legislators and their staff sighed after the visitors departed. Yet, it seemed the minute one contingent left, the congressperson's secretary would be ushering in another bunch. They never seemed to stop coming; hour after hour their accumulating presence spoke urgency, action. They would no longer listen to the usual excuses, instead, insisting, if not in these exact words: "No more bullshit or excuses or blaming institutional lethargy."

It didn't help the legislators' peace of mind that while inside talking with the visitors, the incumbents could hear the roars of the rhythmic drumbeats, "Resign, Resign, Resign, Resign, Resign, Resign," coming from the assembled masses on the back Capital lawn. For all they knew, their visitors would be going outside to join the shouters as soon as they left the Congressional offices.

The Reporter Keeps Spelunking
While the Masses Get Arty

Such a tidal wave of visits, along with all the other new developments, began to have a haunting effect on the solons. The "other developments" included the gentle pressure of the AAC, the rat-crazed media, the coming out of the Speaker—who knew he was a "closeted Commie," as Tush Limba, who uses our public airwaves free to make millions of dollars yearly, put it—there were the approaching primary battles, the demanding editorials, and, especially, the volcanic eruption of the Cooperators' agenda, which was now being widely publicized, and its immense popularity measured both by incessant polls and e-mails, telephone calls, and letters. There were also those demands for meetings from their constituencies, coming from what they would have to call the "unusual suspects," meaning people who had never been heard from before. At this stage, what you had were five hundred and thirty-five lawmakers looking for survival, for any way out and any stratagem that would turn the popular tide from enmity to admiration.

The Reporter caught these dynamic strains on the members and noted that these were new experiences for them. The old slogans, assurances, the intimidating campaign cash hoards and manipulation of patriotic and religious symbols were not only not working; they were backfiring, earning ridicule not acquiescence, ending up causing self-destructive blowback.

It was the Reporter who characterized the legislators' new state of mind with such accuracy and trenchancy that the politicians had to be impressed. After reading the Reporter's latest articles, which seemed to peer into their souls, instead of avoiding him as they used to, they were calling him up for interviews. They also wanted to pick his brain as to what he felt was heading their way on the fast track. The Editor provided two interns to help the Reporter handle all the requests. As he saw it, the more the legislators came to depend on the Reporter, the more inside information would come his way.

The most frequent question legislators put to the Reporter was, "What do you think all those corporate lobbying firms, the trade associations, and the powerful Chamber of Commerce are going to do about what is happening?"

To his mind, one of the lawmakers' underlying fear was that the spigots of lobbyist-sponsored campaign cash and resources, so called fact-finding junkets to places with good golf courses, and other perks would be abruptly turned off. Rather than allay that fear, the Reporter merely called it as he saw it. "There's a good chance the lobbyists, trade associations, and other such organizations will lie low so as not to be caught in the tsunami. Some overdue restored redistribution of wealth they can take in their stride. Some wildly popular law and order motions, especially targeted at egregious corporate wrongdoing, they cannot visibly oppose. Only when they feel their wealth and acquisitions personally are being expropriated or confiscated will they behave like the proverbial cornered rat, stand on their hind legs, and fight.

"Remember, corporations are expedient, opportunistic. When they have to, they'll adjust. That's a lesson from American history. Whenever Congress meant business, business backed off to avoid worse, so as not to let the public think they were as vulnerable as they really were."

For the congresspeople the Reporter spoke with, this message was hardly reassuring, especially as he made no mention of whether this would affect their perks. Personally, the Reporter quite enjoyed watching the way those he was chatting with on the Hill squirmed whenever the back door protesters got particularly loud.

Truthfully, the hourly "Resign, Resign, Resign, Resign, Resign, Resign," was becoming a little tedious for the listeners, though individual town criers didn't do this shouting out for hours, but rather took things in turn as the organizers would rotate fresh criers from the large influx of people into their nation's Capital.

They also started to break the monotonous drill by featuring prominent artists singing songs of rebellion, of no more war but peace, and of unionism. The first celebrity volunteer on stage was Patti Smith who sang, with the crowd joining for every word, her famous composition "The People Have the Power" several times in one day. She insisted on inviting any member of Congress or their staff who was listening to join with them. To the astonishment of the assemblage, several dozen lawmakers and assistants came down from their offices to lend their lungs and lock swaying arms. Other singers followed with their own famous renditions.

This addition of famed artists to the lineup attracted a different kind of media: the entertainment and celebrity reporters who reached actual and virtual audiences rarely touched by even the most vibrant political demonstrations. Such celebrity performances also attracted fans, some of whom, feeling they couldn't really enjoy the music of their favorite singers and bands unless the experience was "enhanced" with some libations, became unruly when they became tipsy. The police made some arrests. Other provocations were not so easily explained, leading the organizers to suspect the authorities were using the old technique of infiltrating the crowd with deliberate provocateurs, who would bring the police swarming in when they created a disturbance. So far, organizers had good relationships with the Capital Police, the DC Police, and the Park Service. There seemed to be no evidence of the casually dressed informants or agitators that anti-war rallies used to attract, in years past sent over by the FBI. Just in case, however, the organizers began "deputizing" young, strong, alert people to be informal sentinels, who would nip brewing trouble in the bud.

Along with talking to those who now held the power, the Reporter, getting antsy, wanted to interview some of the primary challengers who were tearing up the hustings and who soon enough may be power brokers themselves. If they were elected in droves, which was not inconceivable, it would represent the second eviction of the current lawmakers from their offices.

He journeyed to some of these new faces, selecting two challengers in a Kansas Congressional District. One was taking on the incumbent, Republican Danforth Dufur, in the primary and the other, as a Democrat, was set to run against Dufur in the November election. Strangely enough, to the Reporter, these erstwhile opponents seemed downright chummy. The Reporter asked how could this be since there were on different sides of the electoral and ideological aisles.

"We have something very important in common," smiled the primary challenger, "and it's not our great hairdos."

"It's a secret society," teased the November challenger, "with tentacles everywhere."

Not sure he was hearing this right, the Reporter took the bait. "What's that?"

The primary fellow answered for both of them "We both belong to a small select organization around the country. It has no staff. All it has is a name and an indomitable spirit."

He bit on this one too. "So, what's its name?"

"It's called Ousters United in Time or, mellifluously enough, OUT," exclaimed the Primary Challenger. "Each of us has agreed that we need a new agenda, something like the one the Cooperators are working on.

Our first task is to give permanent layoffs to the entrenched waddling around Congress at the moment."

His Democratic friend continued the discourse. "We can't lose. If my bud doesn't win the primary, he'll have left Dufur in such a weakened condition, that I'll simply be administering the coup de grace at election time."

"It's like tag team wrestling," the primary person ended with a flourish.

Although the Reporter would have had to admit, if pressed, he wasn't all that familiar with that gentle sport of pro wrestling, he found the comparison quite appropriate.

Everywhere he traveled, the Reporter witnessed a similar confident élan and a sharing of resources between supposed opponents. Everywhere the tumult of the masses was providing the backdrop for the challenger's brazen boldness. Those running in elections acted audaciously because the public dared them to.

The Reporter's three-part series, in which he detailed the spirit and strategies of the challengers, raised the fright index to stuck-in-a-haunted-house level on Capitol Hill. But the public reaction was almost gleeful, with some comments reflecting the prevailing determination among them, which could have been put into words as: "Whoever wins, they're going to be taking orders from 'we the people.'"

The Rats and their Handlers

As a sidebar, the Reporter updated the public on what had happened to the white mice in cages that the two eighteen-wheelers delivered to the Congress for each member's office. They didn't last long in their new digs. Within a day, however, they were collected by an accommodating chain pet store and put up for sale. However, that was not the end of the white mouse saga.

Daily, visitors to the Congress carried caged white mice, some under cover in large tote bags and others in plain sight, right through the x-ray machine and past the guards. Since pets were allowed into the Capitol, the police did not know how to stop them.

Their Chief went to see the Administration Committee Chairs, who in turn called in the House and Senate parliamentarians.

"What can we do without arousing the animal rights and welfare lobby?" asked one leading senator, a guy who was said to leave no interest group without a nod, and the request for a donation.

One of his staff told him, "The House parliamentarian said that they could conceivably get legislation passed that would bar 'mice,' from accompanying visitors. But, and you know these parliamentarians are all lawyers, they say there would be a problem of definition. You'd logically have to include rats, but how about other rodents such as voles, hamsters, or woodchucks?"

The congressman at the discussion threw up his hands. "Whatever we did, we'd look like fools as well as anti-pet. There's no label that will destroy your career faster than being called anti-pet, a person who doesn't like cats, dogs or even guinea pigs is pilloried. It's worse than being labeled a Red."

"And can you imagine," the senator added, "how this will feed the cartoonists a five star dinner? Imagine when *Doomsbury* gets ahold of it."

"You're probably right," replied the Senate parliamentarian, who was, indeed, a lawyer, "too narrow a definition would be an animal bill of attainder, that is, it would deny singled-out species their day in court, and too broad would be inviting charges of animal abuse, especially if the humans claim that the pet rodents perform as 'service' creatures, something like seeing-eye dogs though, obviously, offering more intangible benefits."

The House parliamentarian paused in what he was saying, holding up a hand to indicate he still had more to say, and raising an eyebrow, he contemplated something that had just come to him in a "light bulb" moment. He resumed, "We could, maybe, stop this scandalous rat-toting by having the rodents declared a public health threat. For the Congressional medical clinics to impose a quarantine is well within their discretionary authority.

"Presto," said the senator. "That's why I keep saying we need more of these brainstorming sessions to handle the all these new challenges ... and challengers."

"Perfecto," said the relieved congressman, though, since he was

Ralph Nader

removing a cigar from his vest pocket, it was unclear whether he was referring to the solution or the brand.

Both rushed to the doctors, with their demand that pet rats be declared risk factors. The prudent doctors said they would have to check the science before deciding anything.

And while that checking went on over endless days and delays—the Ides of March had come and gone—there were more visitors, more pet mice and more consternation among the denizens of Capitol Hill encircled by omnipresent press corps eagerly updating their rat stories. And, without any takers, brazen press photographers asked the congresspeople to pose with the pet rats.

The Cooperators Step Up their Game

Not many blocks away, as the Capitol-ists endured visits from rat-carrying constituents, Doug's group was working furiously as if every day was a deadline. The Cooperators had lined up the most proficient, action-starved citizen groups and think tanks as crews to work on crafting basic legislation covering the necessities of life for the American people. The categories were many: 1) Food, 2) Housing, 3) Energy, 4) Health, 5) Safety, 6) Transportation, 7) Communication, 8) Insurance, 9) Credit, 10) Security, 11) Taxation, 12) Public Works, 13) Children, 14) Retirement/Pensions, 15) Education, 16) Leisure/Play/Art, 17) Work/Wages, 18) Civil Rights/Civil Liberties, 19) Street and Corporate Crime Prevention/Enforcement, 20) Environment, 21) Clean Public Funded Elections with Choice, 22) People Empowerment, 23) Community and Self-Reliance, and 24) Corporation Accountability.

All these laws were put forward within a broad frame of political, economic, and social philosophy, one which drew from the best of both left and right traditions. For example, to conservatives who might view the numerous categories as invitations to expansive government, which, they might feel, was meddling in the polity with no limits, they offered a paper by a prominent legal philosopher, in which he described the two pillars of freedom: *Freedom To* fulfill human possibilities and *Freedom From* arbitrary and abusive power whether public or private in its sourcing. Using these as guiding principles, the philosopher explained how the new laws in multiple areas would enhance these two goods.

Meetings between Cooperator personnel and the more than one hundred sympathetic members of Congress and/or their staff were daily and intense. Everybody knew that time was of the essence; the plutocrats and the oligarchs were caught off guard, but it would not be long before they would develop a multi-faceted counter-attack. Before they did so, the Cooperators were trying to put those opposing them on the defensive. In war and in politics, it comes down to who is seen to be on the offensive and who is put on the defensive. Fence sitters decide which side to back according to their understanding of which side is pushing forward and which giving ground. This perception of who is pushing and who is retreating is acutely judged on Capitol Hill; and according to what they perceive, they shape their behavior, their expectations, their very daily identity. The lawmakers know immediately on any issue who is on the offense and who is on the defense. At this crucial juncture, the people were decidedly on the offense. History—and we know Doug and many of the Cooperators were profound students of history—shows the people do not usually get a second strike opportunity if they muff the first.

A key part of keeping up the pressure and maintaining the offense was keeping the object of struggle in the public eye by putting up posters and carrying placards, physically and on the Internet, that contained a set of common sense, democratic slogans. What the innovators were demanding was not exactly exotic or alien to American capabilities or expectations. The US has a heritage of democratic rebuffs to the fat cats. The visitors roaming Washington, DC, in ever greater numbers, had come up with a particularly juicy poster slogan, referring back to that heritage, though some criticized it as unglamorous and less radical than it might have been, given the scope of change demanded by the general public.

Hundreds of placards were carrying the words: NO BIG DEAL— WE'VE EARNED IT, WE'LL GET IT! The exact phrasing resonated for anyone with a modest knowledge of American history.

Ralph Nader

This was not Franklin Delano Roosevelt's NEW DEAL; it was not Harry Truman's FAIR DEAL; nor was it Lyndon B. Johnson's THE GREAT SOCIETY. It was just NO BIG DEAL! Which could be easily translated into this demand: Get it over with, put civic spirited people in office, and let us live better lives utilizing the resources we've already earned, already produced, ones that have been taken from us aggressively for over half a century.

Plutocrats Are Not Sitting Idle

Where some in the public were grumbling that the No Big Deal slogan was not sufficiently radical, this was hardly something conceivable to the mighty ones who assembled at a very private meeting of DC-based trade associations, with leaders from the US Chamber of Commerce, the National Association of Manufacturers, and numerous more specialized trade groups such as Big Pharma and the Grocery Manufacturers Association.

As a whole, they had grown impatient waiting for signals from Wall Street and the rest of the financial industry. So they had called on a prominent political consultant, Hedrick Van Duke, to hear his thoughts on what was happening and how to proceed.

Van Duke, flashing his famed gold-plated lighter as he lit a cigarillo, said, "Gentlemen, it's too early to call this one. It's hard to say whether this is a tough, larger version of Occupy Wall Street, which will make as much noise and disappear just as quickly—and, note, some people have been leaving town and going back home due to lack of housing—or, given that it is focusing, unlike the Wall Street Occupiers, on specific legislation and legislators, it will have legs." He went on to mention that the big labor unions were not too excited about what was happening and not particularly connected to the street people. He ended, "I have been paying particular attention to union communications and, if my reading of the tea leaves is correct, these organizations' lack of interest is a sign that nothing major is likely to happen." He drew deeply and satisfyingly on his smoke.

Interestingly, Van Duke, who was looking to all his usual channels for information, didn't seem to know much about Doug's busy group and the connections they were making. He thought what Doug's cohorts were doing was nothing more than street theater.

After he concluded, the trade groupies stood up. They had been reassured by Van Duke that these will-of-wisp protests were nothing more than "monkey business as usual," although they did have to recognize there were apostates in their camp: the one hundred dissenting lawmakers and the isolated "switcheroo of a Speaker," as one called him.

As the meeting was taking a coffee and cigarillo break, a guy from Big Pharma cornered a rather shady looking lobbyist. He asked, "Have there been any 'agitators' in the crowds making trouble and tarnishing the so-called peaceful claims of the organizers?"

"Not as of yet," said the lobbyist, Cyrus Searchey, with a knowing wink. Then he added, "but stay tuned."

After an hour of further discussion, the Chairman of the Chamber of Commerce, Albert Ascension, adjourned with the admonition: "Stay alert, stay in touch with each other, and keep writing checks to the politicos. This is a time we need the wheels especially well greased."

Preemptive Foiling

Unbeknownst to the Corporatists, there was a mole in the room, a bespectacled young man who parted his hair down the middle and kept smiling and nodding while others were speaking. He made sure to keep close to Cyrus Searchey.

Afterward, he headed straight to Doug's office to relate what he had heard. Doug was most troubled by the "stay tuned" remark about infiltrators than anything else that was reported. He decided on a little preventive disinformation. Two days later at the daily Resign Shout-Out, a burly, middle-aged white man began pushing people around demanding that the massed gathering storm the Congress,

Ralph Nader

loudly exclaiming, "This is our Bastille! What are we waiting for? Sack the Congress! Sack the Congress! Pitchforks everybody!"

The police moved in and, finding a tear gas canister on him, quickly arrested him for disturbance of the peace and inciting to violence. When asked whether he was acting alone or part of a conspiracy, he was said to have blurted out, "I have to make a living." The remark was duly reported by the police reporters, and was played up in the press and on the evening television, under such heads as "Police catch outside, paid agitator, bent on sabotaging the peaceful assemblage."

Doug turned off the TV, satisfied that the "stay tuned" promise was effectively undermined for the time being.

Billionaires Cabal

To keep abreast of the progress of the movement, the three billionaires got together at Happy's penthouse condo, high over Pennsylvania Avenue. All agreed that providing a consistent, audited money flow to Doug's group and others around the country was a key reason these people were making things happen that would not have happened, and faster and with a better focus to boot. There was no time wasted fundraising and worrying about squalid *quid pro quos*, where a donor expected some favor for giving money. And there was still plenty of money left. But that was not foremost on their minds as they started on their appetizer of shrimp and hot tomato sauce.

The game player began, "When I play chess, which I often do, I try to think a few moves ahead, looking out for trouble down the road. For Doug and others, I anticipate them having problems when they bring up any bills that take on the 'military-industrial complex,' which President Eisenhower warned us about. The President's original draft, by the way, said the 'military-industrial-Congressional complex.' But let me get back to what I foresee as our hidden advantage in this particular fight.

"Something rather unprecedented happened during the year-long run-up to war on Iraq orchestrated by Bush and Cheney from 2002–

2003. Go back as far as you want in our history, all the way back to the Revolutionary War period that Happy is always on about, and you will never find an another example of what went on this time during the drumbeat period before military action.

"Over three hundred retired generals, admirals, very-high-ranking officers, national security officials, presidential advisors, and diplomats, who had worked either for Republican or Democratic administrations, individually came out openly and publically against the pending invasion of a country that never threatened us. They gave their reasons in op-eds, interviews, letters to the editor, joint statements, and meetings.

"Here's the second striking thing. It was an opportunity lost. The supine and at that point largely jingoistic press, understandably did not dwell on these anti-invasion statements from military men and women. And when not much happened, these dispersed critics went back home.

"At the same time, one other person was speaking and writing against this reckless war-mongering, which was mired in falsehoods, deceptions, and secrecy. He was the famous mega-billionaire Thomas Toros. Here's where a tremendous, hope-laden option was missed. Indeed, it's one of the reasons I signed onto Happy's program with such enthusiasm. Because, as I see it, if Toros had provided paid national media, a secretariat, and other supporting infrastructure, the three hundred lone and separated voices would have become one thousand in a month. The White House juggernaut of propaganda and captive media and the compliant, cowed Congress would have faced a formidable challenge. The concocted war-time illusion by the White House would have dissolved like a mummy hitting air. It would be gone the way a nightmare is when we wake up.

"After that time, I often daydreamed about what would have happened if Toros or, to be more candid, if I myself, had chipped in a few millions to get the three hundred high visibility. The president and his advisors, the Congress and the media would have been thrown on the defensive, losing momentum by the day. Who could have faced down an organized phalanx of such a retired, patriotic, experienced, war-tested group of Americans with no axe to grind, indeed, asking us to collectively put down our axes, in interviews and testimony given daily at the local, state and national level?"

The happy-go-lucky rich man got the picture. "Instead of regretting

Ralph Nader

what might have been, we can use the outlines that our chess-playing friend just mentioned as a road not taken. Thomas Toros is still around and active. Since he was so outspoken against the war machine, couldn't he be called upon again? And we can also resurrect hundreds of these retired people and their like-minded successors to bring down the power of this warring complex."

The libertarian didn't want them to go off half-cocked and asked, "What if Thomas Toros remains as reluctant as he was in 2002-2003 to provide the treasure?"

The chess player would not give up his vision so easily. "If Toros doesn't man up, then I will spend my own money."

Happy remarked, "You know we and our money are behind this. It's something I've noticed as things have progressed. We have been finding many great, democratically attuned people who possess in abundance the necessary skills in public relations, writing, and research. There are plenty around, having waited and waited years with unused knowledge for such an opportunity. I feel the same about my money. It's been sitting idle for years, waiting for just such a chance to help with the accomplishment of great things."

The libertarian laid out the immediate tasks, beginning with, "Okay, it looks like we're on the same page. Let's make the calls to the more prominent retired military people and peace-spirited money men and women, who then can each bring in their own circle. We'll need to make assignments to our action staff to get it done. As the cliché goes, 'It's not rocket science.'"

With that, they set off on the more lighthearted portion of the evening, eating a scrumptious dinner and exchanging commentary on the amazing phenomenon unfolding before them.

Hear, Hear

The All American Caucus had a seminal meeting, which they all attended with their legislative calendars in each hand. Now numbering one hundred and ten and calling themselves all "Co-Chairpersons," the members agreed that the next order of business was to press for prompt Congressional hearings for each item on their tables and the Cooperators' agenda. Fortunately, the logisticians among them had found that there were many under-challenged Congressional committees and sub-committees with readily available hearing rooms and budgets.

Of course, AAC members, doing a little of the carefully articulated anticipation the chess player spoke about, realized that stopping a bill in the hearing was a traditional way to block any action since the routine was that no piece of legislation, except for refueling the country's boomeranging wars such as in Iraq and Afghanistan, could go to the floor without prior hearings. With this in mind, the AAC wanted hearings for reasons of professionalism and to take away the excuses of obstructionists and their lobbying friends, who, if the AAC had tried to put a bill on the floor before it had been vetted in hearings, would have cried foul, labeling the process unfair, precipitous, and authoritarian.

Although as Committee Chairs, conservative legislators were reluctant to hold hearings, they were swayed not only by the clamoring inside the buildings of the AAC caucus but by the clamor arising outside when the "Resign, Resign" crowds started chanting, "Hearings, Hearings." Their voices reverberated and were repeated throughout the congresspeople's districts back home. The chairs of the committees, no matter their positions, felt they had no choice but to schedule hearings for ten straight days, allowing only one week advance notice for preparations and witnesses. Obviously, weekends were cancelled and all hands were on deck.

The media was relieved. Reporters did not like how demonstrators and many in the public had taken to calling them "Rat Reporters" or "journalists on the Rat Beat"

It demeaned them even though all this political discontent and protesting sold papers and got high TV/radio ratings. They were sick of being assigned to reporting on these tedious government news conferences, in which they were asked to be no more than conduits, presenting the official view to the public. They were ready for substance and the clash of interest groups.

Ralph Nader

Their editors, seeing the public was hungry for this news, reassigned business and style pages reporters, along with some sports reporters and columnists, to join and bolster their colleagues on Capitol Hill covering the hearings. These men and women, having become bored feeding the masses' once-insatiable desire for gossip and sports stats, were more than glad to be freed from their daily drudgery to join in conveying to the American people, and the world, what was going on during these historic days of action, drama, of serious purpose. As would happen with most anyone, the prospect of significance, that is, the fact that what they did might make some valuable imprint on the world, elevated their feelings of professional self-regard and competence. Before this historic opening, the newspeople's marketing of trivia, repetition, and other dreary formulaic routines was feeding a work attitude of just "put in your time," then retire.

For members of the committees and their staffs the hearings were a new occupational experience. No more restricting their activities within the "Tuesday to Thursday Club," with members taking leave of their duties and going home or on other trips from Friday to Monday afternoon. They were on a seven-day week, forced to show up for work by the spotlight trained on them by millions of agitating citizens back home, and by a de-stupefied social media as well as by, closer to home, the large crowds around the Capitol. And, in the newest wrinkle of the protestors' tactics, sleek town cars incessantly circulated around outside the Congress with signs and bullhorns.

Once committee hearings were scheduled and their times posted, long lines, starting at dawn, formed outside the House and Senate Office Buildings as the common people sought entrance into the limited seats of the hearing rooms. This was not going to be the usual fill-'em-up-with-lobbyists unless, that is, the lobbyists themselves—no paid stand-ins—were willing to line up in the cold at 5 am and wait for four hours till the doors opened.

The Reporter, who was covering the hearings and the lines, noticed that the lobbyists' customary ploy, hiring young men and woman at twenty dollars an hour to stand in line for them until the hearing room opens, at which time the lobbyists sauntered in to take their place in line, was not working. The street ralliers had warned the lines against such usurpations, so that now crowds identified such substitutes and politely ushered them away.

Once inside, and after the committee and sub-committee chairs had gaveled open the hearings, the Reporter found another departure from business as usual. The witnesses, often in panels, were distinctly unrepresentative of the tight circle of professional testifiers from corporatist think tanks, trade groups, and compensated "experts," on corporate retainers, who usually dominated the witness stand. Average people spoke during these sessions, put forth by back-home populist politics. They related the experience, expectations, and demands of usually forgotten, excluded, disrespected ,and over-charged people. It was a veritable citizens' army of the harmed, underpaid, uninsured, pension-stripped, job-insecure, workers. Those chosen to represent were unbowed; they were the thinkers and doers unbound and free to speak truth.

The chairs, forced to accommodate such plain speakers, were happy when, having given them a fair say, they were able to call on the characters they were more accustomed to listening to: the "suits," the well heeled who had tongues well oiled. Yet, both the chairs and the watching Reporter saw that something was wrong. The lobbyists and corporate flaks presented their views, but the calm exhibition of command was not there. The overall climate in the country seemed to have discouraged them from coming out so complacently with their usual warnings that if anything was touched in the business world there would be massive layoffs, companies would move abroad, or lose the incentives to produce.

Yet even with largely toned-down presentations of their business-first views, which called for standing pat on all the present, cozy arrangements, there was a clear contrast between what they stood for and claimed, and what the rest of the population challenged and knew. It was really no contest. And everybody in those hearing rooms and the vast audience streaming outside recognized that change. Whether elated or biting their lips, no one could assert, moreover, that there were inadequate public records, or working models, that brought out the facts involved in each subject area, and which were supplied by AAC staffers. During the hearings, there were plenty of cross-examinations, and filings which had gone into the committees' records for public discussion in all the media.

Ralph Nader

They Keep On Ticking

As the hearings continued, the Reporter became intensely curious about the stamina of the people clamoring daily everywhere. So many pundits had predicted that the public's burnout was just around the corner that he wondered what kept them going, seemingly on an upward curve by which it appeared their involvement was continually expanding, not flagging as so often has happened to other movements over the decades. Since the hearings and the background stories were being covered by hundreds of reporters, and, as we know, the Reporter didn't like to hunt with the pack, he asked his editor to send him around the country for a whirlwind ten days so he could try to fathom this remarkable civic constancy.

The Reporter's first stops were the bus lines. He Greyhounded it across the land, listening in to the small talk of the passengers. People were talking about how the demonstrations for this and that change were going to make their personal families lives better. Others were on their way in clusters to marches and rallies and city council hearings. Even the high-schoolers were looking at each other (instead of looking at their iPhones) as they talked over the rising possibility of their getting free college educations and high minimum wages for their part-time jobs.

The Reporter filed his first story, giving it the title: "Small Talk Down; Big Talk Rises." It was chocked with quotes he had overheard from his fellow bus-riders. He captured the spontaneity and emotion of the common folk in a far better way than was ever done in a stilted "man in the street" interview.

Next stop on his explorations were the diners and crowded fast food eateries. In them, he heard arguments about substantive proposals before Congress. He was surprised to hear that the speakers often evinced considerable knowledge of the subjects, more perhaps than that possessed by congress members. It reminded him of what he had read about the serious talk among the Texas farmers in 1886–1888 when they were debating the sub-treasury plan, which they were supporting as a way to give them reasonable credit, allowing them to escape the clutches of the banks.

It persuaded the Reporter, as he wrote in a second article, that when people give themselves a chance to read, talk, and think, they can, even in this flashy, sound-bite media age, rise to the occasion. He put in his story a quote from a 20th century organizer who, when asked why she fought so hard for democracy, replied, "Because it brings the best out of people."

His next dispatch was based on his visits to the teeming student populations, heavily minority, whom he found attending California's large community colleges. He quickly learned that students were cutting their vocational classes so they could hear open-air speakers discussing the current democratic revival or to attend workshops for pending actions demanding big changes in how the country was run.

Previously, for a piece he did on this level of education, the Reporter had noticed, that mostly from low-income families, community college students were all about the business of enhancing their employment prospects. Apart from some charitable activity, there seemed to be little civic awareness or activity on campus, at least when he filed his story two years ago. That seemed along ago, for there had been a sea change in campus opinion. The new dispensation was striking. It is as if the new political discourse had allowed students to articulate a sense of injustice in relation to their families' anxious plight in the inequitable economy, which galvanized them, finally putting muscle in the designation of their schools as for "community."

As the Reporter made his rounds, he noticed, further, that student involvement in civic actions was having a psychological effect. Activism and showing up for gatherings, rallies and meetings was the thing to do, and, as this continued, the experiences had become internalized so that everyone counted on everybody to pull together as part of the local culture. Not turning out for a demonstration was frowned upon. The mavericks were the apathetic people.

In his fourth article, the Reporter alluded to the ancient city of Athens where the word "idiot" referred to residents of that remarkable town who did not engage in Athenian democracy. They shirked their citizen duties, and so were labeled ignorant, self-isolated, and not public citizens.

Idealists throughout the centuries have looked back to those ancient

Ralph Nader

Athenians (although they restricted women and other subdued groups from full participation) as ideal insofar as it was a city-state where peer group pressure bent towards public, civic engagement and reproached people who withdrew into their individual selfishness. They saw voluntary, self-motivated engagement as a collective survival practice.

The Reporter had a talent for weaving in such historic references to older state forms into his daily narratives, giving them context and gravity.

In his final wrap-up article on visiting engaged people across the nation, he described the emerging culture of civic-ism finding roots in the psyche, the status, the self-actualization of many people who lost their fear and worry. He noted that people such as these were often making history but did not realize it, and if they did, they would push forward with even more force and profoundity.

Common people reading his now-celebrated reports felt pride. Uncommon people, namely, the oligarchs felt dread. They gritted their teeth and hunkered down with the belief that corporate stamina would eventually outlast these public outrages. So, they had to be careful not to overplay their hands. Refusing to bend, they could indeed be broken. Bending became their present tactical mantra.

Little things began to worry these ruling cliques. There was an exchange of words from several high-schoolers waiting for their bus. It went viral. Three students were overheard chattering about some politicians' voting records. A couple of students, laughing, told them, "They were not turned on to politics," and urging them to come to a dance that night at the Y. The serious student replied, "Don't you remember your history courses? Wherever people anywhere in the world were not turned on to politics, politics turned on them in a vicious, cruel way."

"Activism by the young has become 'cool,'" concluded the Reporter.

People's Democracy, Could It
Be Good For Business?

Back at the Congressional hearings, the chairs had to frequently admonish witnesses to offer their specific opinions on the pending legislation and not grandstand. The major bills that called for big changes were, not surprisingly, those supported by the grassroots, the Cooperators, and the AAC. The designated numbers of the bills—HR This and S That—were already all over the social media and on posters and placards carried by the marchers and held aloft at the rallies. Copies of the bills were brought by constituents with their visits to Congress, perhaps stuffed in a pocket on the side of their pet rat cages. The AAC didn't object to the filing of other bills related to each subject, nefarious bills which negated or weakened their agenda; bills expertly contrived by the corporate law firms. While the AAC would fight tooth and nail against these bits of legislation, it was part of the AAC's design to take away all possible excuses by their opponents by giving them full right to introduce any noxious legislation they wanted.

A pleasant surprise for the AAC and a source of groans for the hardliners were the testimonies of enlightened, recently formed, ad hoc business organizations whose corporate executives took offense at the US Chamber of Commerce presuming to speak for them as if all of business was of one mind against introducing major changes.

These witnesses attracted media attention and profiles as they came out in favor of equitable taxation; a more lean, efficient defense, not a bloated offensive military; and with public spirited environmental, consumer and labor positions. As a whole, they were arguing that the evidence overwhelmingly proved that the stronger a democracy is, the more prosperous and productive it is. As one executive put it, "To have a robust economy it's a simple matter of higher wages, larger consumer demand, better public services, superior business ideas, and the security and fairness of the law."

While these testimonies were irksome to the corporate boosters, they were gratifying to the three billionaires, since they indicated that fellow businessmen and women were hearing the message of reform that the trio had harkened to early on. The three of them were forthright in urging forward and facilitating the presence of these good business groups.

One evening, gathered in Happy's Washington penthouse over drinks, the start-up backer read to his chums a passage from one of his favorite thinkers, the British philosopher/mathematician of the early twentieth century Alfred North Whitehead, to wit: "The behavior of the community is largely dominated by the business mind. A great society is a society in which its men of business think greatly of their functions. Low thoughts mean low behavior, and after a brief orgy of exploitation low behavior means a descending standard of life."

"Very impressive," responded the libertarian.

"Very motivational," declared the chess player, "especially for us who are thinking 'greatly of our functions,' which boil down to fighting to give the people a deciding vote in how business and politics are conducted."

It had come to this. They, behind the scenes players, were ready to step into the limelight alongside these other progressive business people. Duly instructed, their "action man" made it happen. It turned out not to be that difficult. They were ready to make their voices heard on prime time.

The entrance of alternative business advocacy groups upset the equations of power in Washington. Over the years, the mainline, old trade lobbies had succeeded in forging a remarkable unity. They almost always did speak with one voice, even turning the large National Federation of Independent Business into a dependency that slavishly followed the big business line. Whistleblowers, players who got sick of the fixed game and spoke out, were few and subject to a dedicated retaliation of discrediting and blacklisting. Now, to the consternation of conservative trade agencies, along came the various issue-oriented business groups speaking their own minds, writing op-eds, giving national television interviews, and applying their great expertise with the social media, greater than that possessed by the old line groups due to their mostly younger leaders. With business unity so broken, "Would Humpty Dumpty," as one pundit put it, "ever be put back together again?" Or, in the whining words of Tush Limba, "Did even Hercules have to deal with such a Hydra?"

Washington and Wall Street Face Off

The entrenched business lobbies were perplexed and did not know what they could counter with other than mere repetition of their arguments. Never before had they faced such treachery in their own camp. There were no ideologically alien "isms" to taint their rising corporate tormentors with, nor could they accuse them of not meeting payrolls or not being innovative or profitable or of acting to undermine capitalism. How could these entrenched business lobbies cast aspersions on these fellow businessmen when they themselves were vulnerable to attack in that they themselves were immersed in demanding subsidies and being instrumental in creating the crony capitalism so hated by both left and right. Who were they to be righteous? Meanwhile, in a maddening way, they saw the upstart business groups set up shop in Washington for the long term as if they had no plans of going away.

It was high time for one more confidential strategy session where the Washington lobbies went to New York to size up the situation with, what they called pejoratively, the "Wall Street Crowd." The Washington trade lobbies felt that if they were culpable in small ways, such as by asking for handouts, the very nature of Wall Street business—making big money from pension funds, mutual funds, and small investor money in ever more destabilizing, speculative ways—was much more objectionable. Wall Street made more profits by this rampant speculation than those making real things and offering real service could ever hope to see. But the indiscriminate American public, really sickened by Wall Street shenanigans, tended to paint all business with a broad brush.

The chronic tension between the two business blocs is not widely known because of the way it has been effectively contained by the well-oiled public relations firms. Since Wall Street collapsed on the entire economy in the great recession in 2008–2009, the resentment has worsened. The Washington trade groups and their members back home rightfully fear that the "too big to fail" banks are still with us, and still addicted to playing dangerous games with people's money. According to the trade groups, these goliath banks and their reckless financial circles have not learned their lesson. They are continuing their risky speculations, especially with multi-tiered derivatives (bets on bets on bets) that could, once again, sink all businesses and bring on Uncle Sam's overzealous bailouts. Still, as they filed into the great conference room with its majestic mahogany table, the Washington lobbies had to put their best face on the situation and swallow their antagonisms to concentrate. It's no time to quibble when you are facing a tidal wave.

The rarely agitated Chairman seemed agitated now, greeting the arrivals as colleagues in distress. "Ladies and Gentlemen, pardon the strict security procedures and the frisking of all cell phones and other metallic and plastic objects on your person. It was done for the good and safety of all of us. I don't want to alarm anyone, and we have nothing to worry about this time, but I have reason to believe our last meeting was attended by a hostile mole.

"Now let's get down to business and hear first from our guests. I understand you have appointed good spokespersons. Please proceed."

Rising to speak was a middle-aged gentleman, sporting a large US flag button, known to them all as the leading spokesman for the US Chamber of Commerce.

"We won't need more than one opening presentation of the crisis confronting us before discussion can commence. The situation is clear. We're facing from the people alone a triumvirate in this onslaught. The three elements of protest are: first, those demonstrating *en masse* day after day back home; second, the huge influx of people pouring into Washington, and organized and funded for an array of tactical show-ups and showdowns, most prominently the RESIGN, RESIGN, RESIGN bellowers at the rear of the Capital, but also those targeting and talking to government agencies and trade associations; and, third, rich people who have come from out of nowhere to provide an endless source of funding to keep this hubbub going.

"I don't have to tell you that inside Congress is an astute, well-orga-nized All American Caucus of some one hundred and ten legislators who have taken the initiative away from our base, which had already been addled by the conversion of Speaker Blamer.

"I also need not remind you that it was the rodent animal kingdom that provoked this whole shebang, but that doesn't remove all responsibility from us. The invasion of the rats upset things, but then the inept over-reaction to their frolic helped enlarge the momentum and the ridicule, which left a deep-imprint memory on people with short attention spans.

"What has really got us worried, certainly, is that these carryings-on are not confined to energetic protests but have been turned into a cluster of bills finely drafted and filed, ones which, if passed, would upend our whole cozy little system. And does anyone think they can't be passed? The public hearings underway are convincing the public of these measures value, and the fear of a primary challenger has weakened the position of many of our most ardent champions. And then there is the time factor. Our opponents have squeezed us so that anything we decide to do will have to be initiated and carried through in an incredibly short time span—no more than a month we estimate. We are unable to either mount a television campaign—for the public is on to us—or counter the momentum that has our allies, if not on the run, then on the defensive or fighting against themselves.

"The train has left the station. The numbers have been counted. All we have been able to come up with are salvage operations, like trying to put a short expiration time leash on the bills or trying to reduce the budgets for enforcing or implementing these bills if they do get enacted or deleting some of the criminal penalties these hotheads want to fix on them. Even these last gap measures are not likely to be adopted. It's like trying to stop a stampede of bulls with cocker spaniels.

"Sorry not to be optimistic but we have to face facts." He fingered his patriotic button as if that talisman would give him some strength. "We're up against, first and foremost, the immediate primary season, and that gives us some spirit as we draw on the survival instincts of the lawmakers. Even so, we know the pitchforks are not coming; they are already here. Crazed rats with pitchforks!"

The Chamber of Commerce speaker mopped his brow and sat down.

The Chairman, who seemed to have lost his agitation—he was a can-do type, who loved handling a crisis, the more dire, the better—now had his work cut out for him. He said to the flag-lapelled previous speaker, "I must say, you are not exaggerating the looming situation confronting us. And it affects we corporate types as deeply as it threatens

Ralph Nader

you, even though you are facing a more immediate catastrophe of being literally unseated from the height of power.

"We are equally affected in that we have long known, have we not, that the strongest source of our global power as businesses has been the Congress? It is through that foremost of the three branches of government, staffed with our people by our noble solons, from whence we achieve the space and lenient laws that allow us to make more of our money. This is just one factor that helps cement together the invincible, synergistic duality of business and government wedded together by the majorities of only five hundred and thirty-five people down there.

"Consider it an all-powerful kind of Khyber Pass. I know you who work on global business are aware that the pass between Afghanistan and Pakistan was the historic gateway for all invaders who wanted to grab the booty from the regions. Alexander the Great went through there as did Genghis Khan. Whoever held that pass held the region.

So, for business to reign in a nation, it has to occupy the metaphoric Kyhber Pass between the people and laws governing the society, which is our august Congress.

"You know what? Just as we have dominated this Khyber Pass to get our way, we can fall if the Khyber Pass is taken over as a channel by which the multitudes get their way. Their activists are beginning to realize, what we all have privately known, that one percent or less of real active citizens is all they need, *provided* public opinion is behind them, to overcome our one percent."

On his scratch pad, the Chamber of Commerce man wrote, "Live by the Khyber Pass. Die by the Khyber Pass."

"Now, to get to the quick," continued the Chairman, "and take a brutal assessment of the situation, which presently is so much in our opponents' favor. To put that in plain terms, let us discuss just how much do we lose over the longer run if the other side triumphs in Congress?"

All around the room, notepads were being filled at a rapid pace.

The Chairman continued, "Much of what makes up the Cooperators' agenda already exists in Western Europe and Canada. We make plenty of money in those countries. Other sets of bills want to simplify the laws and repeal laws that are purposeless but nagging at us. While other legislation gives some balance to labor and consumers to head off the kind of frauds and other violations that give all business a bad name. As far as civil rights and civil liberties, passage of better laws in that sector, which we the corporations take full advantage of daily, helps widen markets and enhances predictability and stability. We have learned that lesson, I hope. Main Street must like the emphasis on community business and self-reliance. Don't we want to be self-reliant in energy? How can we oppose clean elections and civic education? For sure, the overall package forces us to share more, but by so doing, we make more. My thought here is maybe we should be letting the people have the money to spend, that they deserve, and giving them the public services that private capital doesn't want to invest in, though it benefits enormously from them every day. Let's acknowledge those benefits and let them increase while keeping in mind that money in the common people's pockets eventually ends up in our pockets as soon as they consume. And Americans love to consume, piggybanks be damned."

Heads were nodded in agreement over that bon mot.

"That's the national field. But what about foreign policy?" the Chairman continued.

"Lots of us are sick and tired of all these wars that the politicians are getting us into around the world. They stir up ever more violence against our presence all over. And, I'm going to let you in on a little secret. People that hate America don't buy our products.

"My sum-up is their slogan, 'No Big Deal.' It is time to take the longer look."

The Washingtonians blanched and then sucked air.

The Chamber's speaker blurted: "Did I hear what I've just heard?!"

"You damn well did," said the Chairman, who didn't like this fellow's tone.

"I can't believe you're serious. Your speech was nothing short of traitorous. This is Benedict Arnold to the tenth power. This is complete surrender, unconditional surrender, even though you started by inferring it was a hypothetical, and, even now, I dearly hope it was. I can't imagine your distinguished colleagues around the table support you in even raising such a possibility?"

The Chairman smiled expansively. Here was just the sort of challenge he liked. "I don't want to make this a duel between the honorable member of the US Chamber and myself. Let's open things up a little. "Feel free, everybody around the table, to say your piece. After all, that is what a discussion is about."

A New York banking magnate with a dollar sign, in quadruple-plated solid gold, on his lapel, jumped in. "I didn't want to get to where our Chairman went so quickly. But now that we've gone through the Khyber Pass into candor-land, I must share my inner thoughts about our big banks, which have gone right back to speculation and derivatives after nearly destroying the world economy by their let-the-buyer-beware practices in 2008–2009. They are still counting on getting off the hook from the next disaster by becoming even more too big to fail.

"Speaking as one who knows, let me say that we bankers can't resist temptation. If we are not saved from ourselves, next time the collapse will find a fed-up, angry electorate that will call for and get nationalization of the banks, regardless of who is in Congress or the White House. You don't need a crystal ball to see that if that happens, it will be followed by turmoil here and overseas, followed by other takeover demands on other industries tethered to our financial networks. Pitchforks? Hell. This time the rats will be driving bulldozers and pelting us with napalm!"

A New York insurance executive, less personally wealthy, spoke next: "As we all know, when the banks speak, insurance listens. Like younger brothers, we walk in the footsteps of those we consider elder siblings. Bank redlining leads to insurance redlining. We follow the credit and then make the bets. The feds are targeting some of our larger insurance companies as 'too big to fail' and, therefore, subject to more regulation and capital reserve requirements.

"To get to the point, if my friend from a big bank sees that now is the right time for radical reform, I can't help but say the insurance companies are more than willing to follow in the tracks of our financial brothers."

All the Washington spokespersons and their adjuncts were taken aback. This was not what they had expected to hear. The scene was getting out of hand. And while they were breaking out in sweats and fingering their lapel buttons, the Chairman's group was not noticeably upset, at least outwardly.

What they personally hated, almost above all, was the confession of weakness on the part of one of the business community. One attending began, "Are we from two different worlds, here? I can't believe I'm hearing such concessions coming from the very business community that screwed up in 2008 and brought down the economy. Now you're saying you can't help yourself, as if you were chronic drunks or cocaine addicts, and you are asking the government to detoxify you as if you wanted to go into some kind of dirty profit addiction rehab.

"And just to touch on the question of image, I must say that's something you can never say in public, so how are you going to explain your surrender in front of the baying pack of media-hounds?"

A New York corporate attorney, who was known as cooler than cool, said: "Let's calm down. I don't think we're anywhere near the point of talking to the public about these views. It's just a discussion, after all."

He continued. "The business people here are acting as if all is lost. Let me call up another scenario, one you are all familiar with. Just imagine a dire event occurring, one far worse than a handful of rats eating the legislators' lunches. I'm thinking, for example, of a terrorist attack larger than 9/11 or a sudden collapse of a major corporation with far-reaching tentacles like AIG, or a major earthquake or infectious epidemic mega-disaster.

"Now what if we got credible scientists and national security officials to start predicting such likelihoods? You know there are plenty of doom-sayers around, many of them backed by facts. They just need megaphones. Ones we can provide. The distractions they provide can help divert the people's attention. Break their momentum, to give us time"

A New York securities ratings magnate couldn't let that pass. "Counsel, methinks you are a bit too sanguine in thinking such a complex and exposable plan could be worked. I don't even want to question how you would go about getting this accomplished—however legal— without any footprints. Besides, Armageddon-type warnings are a dime-a-dozen. Until it happens, people don't give it a thought. They have their daily burdens to worry about. Look at the Bay Area in California and the certain likelihood of 'the Big One,' the doozy of a quake that has been predicted for years."

"Just a thought," meekly replied the corporate counsel. "I was just running it up the flagpole to see who would salute. Maybe you're right. We shouldn't over-imagine."

He was getting dirty looks.

Despite the fact that no one welcomed the lawyer's comments, his let-it-all-hang-out attitude seemed to have an open sesame effect on the assemblage. Questions and answers darted back and forth like balls in a ping pong game, often not directed at the whole gathering but between adjacently seated business people versus Wall Street types.

Here are some of the quick dialogues.

"You're not ready to oppose higher taxes?" from one unbelieving trade representative.

An adjacent Wall Streeter shot back, "They're not my taxes; they're company taxes or my descendant's taxes. It depends if the money is used wisely for such ends as repairing or building better public facilities, doesn't it?"

Another Chamber of Commerce minion talked about what she thought would be a weak point, "But the corporations will never be persons anymore!"

She got in answer, "So? They never were. The whole idea is sacrilegious." The replying executive was a deeply religious Baptist.

A small business representative raised what he took to be another chink in business people's armor. "You guys will be over-regulated to death."

The answer he got: "Not if we emulate best practices in our respective industries. We'll be ahead of any regulations. Some companies have already followed this line. Look at the Interface Corporation, for example, or the Patagonia Corporation or The Body Shop"

This tit-for-tat exchange went on for twenty minutes between the two groups. Finally, another Washington trade association spokesman stood up and asked for a half-hour recess in an adjoining conference room.

Sensing that this break would be welcomed by everyone, the Chairman sweetly replied, "By all means, friends. Take longer if you wish. But as you talk things over among yourselves, keep in mind the differences between our two groups. You are responding to your dues-paying members who expect you to constantly warn and constantly fight that which you have told them is detrimental to their interests. We are responsible to our shareholders who have no power and seemingly no interest in our lobbying positions as such. You may wish to separate this behavioral difference or motivation, realizing we are given much more leeway by the people who are invested in us than you may be your clients. Frankly, I think that may give us a little more objectivity. Think about that when you repair to your deliberations down the hallway."

Breakout Session Agrees to Disagree and Disaggregate

Spokespeople for different trade organizations grouped together in one smaller conference room. They decided to keep with the no-holds-barred framework that had been operative in the bigger meeting.

A spokeswoman for the retail trades seemed incredulous. "Do you think they are serious or do you think they are testing our mettle? This is just so unlike them that I can't believe it's anything but the latter, though there is a kernel of truth in everything they say. But a kernel is not the cob."

A military weapons industry tradesman spoke sharply, "I hate to disabuse you, but I think they are nearing a belief in what they're saying today. Remember, they've had the shit kicked out of them for several years since the Great Recession. And the daily headlines about their messing up have worn them down.

"Besides, these financial fellows really are different from us, they are part of the paper economy, making funny money from money in a global financial world. They wouldn't know how to make one of their own paperclips. They aren't embedded in the real world the way we are. I don't see why we have to follow them. Maybe it's time we struck out on our own? We're Big Boys and Girls too, and we're tangible."

A Washington corporate lawyer, not the same one who had gone off his rocker in the bigger meeting, hastened to back the last speaker: "You're making good sense. Even if the masses prevail *in the short haul*, there is all kinds of monkey-wrenching we can attach to the legislation in coded language they'll never notice. I'm referring to expiration dates, waivers, exemptions, budget deferrals, dilatory administrative procedures for any enforcement, not to mention what we can pile on the agencies and departments, making sure the heads are our nominees, guys willing, ready, and able to tie up implementation. After all, this is what we do, what we have been doing forever. It's in our DNA. Anytime we lose in Congress, we go to work on the agencies and the courts where we often win—either win on the issues or win by interminable procrastination maneuvers. And as they say in my profession: Time is money."

A timber/lumber mogul nodded his head affirmatively. "OK, what you're talking about is the important Plan B. So you are giving up on Plan A? This appears to mean that we concede the Cooperators' agenda—minus our pesky amendments here and there. Should we go that far or should we still go all out to smash this 'people's' revolt, which is backed by large majorities?"

An agri-business CEO offered, "I think, given the primaries' threat, it is too late to 'nip' anything in the bud or even appear to beat back this tsunami. Just trying will further discredit and disable us, weakening our future influence. Let's admit this is historic in its way and history has not been kind to Tories or southern plantation owners. We would most certainly lose, in any event, and probably help them recruit more activists and more funding and more media for their causes. Our behind-the-scenes activity on Capitol Hill—using arguments like 'Isn't this going a bit extreme?' to win the amendments mentioned by our sagacious counsel—may be the best we can do."

An executive mining magnate was a hard-liner. "Am I in the minority in experiencing disbelief over what I've been hearing earlier and just now? Has the fight gone out of us? I hope I'm not speaking only for myself when I say I don't want to have the 1872 Mining Act repealed, making it so our companies have to start paying royalties to the government from our mines on public lands. We're all affected by this. Can you imagine the environmental mandates, the increase in lawsuits blocking extraction, and the growth of substitute materials that can start putting us out of business?"

"Jack," said a mid-size generic drug company chieftain, "much of what you are declaiming against is happening anyway. You're already in the courts, where you win some and lose some. Trends toward more efficient and renewable materials are not going to be stopped. For heaven's sake, the business magazines where you advertise are trumpeting this 'new industrial wave' repeatedly.

"To be perfectly honest, in my business, we have to sell anti-delusionary medicines to unfortunate patients estranged from reality. Not to push this analogy too far, but institutions are also susceptible to delusionary behavior. Even our pharmaceutical companies are regularly accused of being unreal in our pricing, in our aggressive promotions, in our incessant discoveries of new ailments requiring medicine. Haven't you heard of shaking leg syndrome, which some medical researchers claim is an invention of drug sellers?

"Here in our private inner sanctum, I can admit the people's revolt is drawing us closer to reality and away from our risky delusions or, for that matter, our illusions. I guess you could say I am echoing some of the Chairman's views, but couldn't we look at this rat-sparked rebellion and the movement it spawned as a unique time, the compressed eruption being a giant *reset* of our economy. It's one which, if we handle it right, will keep us still operational within a regulated, competitive market economy or, more precisely, an economy of markets, for many more decades.

"I guess one manifestation of this reset is that we have to internalize and pay for some of the costs we inflict on our customers, our workers and our environment—a responsibility that should lead to more prevention and more innovation. This is a reset of the people's livelihoods in a way that is in accordance with some of our most cherished, longheld values, religious, secular, or otherwise. Sorry for the sermon. End of speech. Hail to the rats!"

While some of the attendees were muttering they had found another traitor in their midst, a leader from the machine tools industry was willing to see some light in this tunnel. She openly addressed the hardliner Jack. "The 1872 Mining Act, which even lets foreign companies find and extract hard rock minerals for free—well, almost, they pay five dollars per acre—is the ultimate example of crony capitalism. Letting a Canadian company get ownership of NINE BILLION DOLLARS of our gold on public lands in Nevada for less than thirty thousand dollars is downright crazeee! What business can be run like that? Only the USA out of all the countries in the world has laws like this that make it such a sucker. You couldn't get ten percent of the American people behind you on that one, Jack."

Magnate Jack came back at her strong, "I beg your pardon. Do you want me to start a list of the crony capitalist arrangements each of you benefits from? We're not here to make a donnybrook and insult each other. I'm sorry I even mentioned the 1872 Act. Let's get back to why we've got a recess. What are we going to say to the Wall Streeters?"

A hospital chain CEO declared, "I keep thinking about the Chairman's parting comments. We do have different constituencies. If we consider the profiles of our organization's members, we see that they pay dues and have influence in their own right. Walls Streeters speculate much, invest less. Our members are concerned with the common people in that we meet their real needs and wants."

"Putting all that together, I don't see any reconciliation toward a united front with the Wall Street types, but I also don't see us going into flat-out, public opposition. We can go back to them down the hall and tell them this."

"As for us, I suggest each trade association do their own thing, as they see fit. Our most immediate concern now has to be keeping friendly legislators in office. Based on their own needs, let each of us speak to legislators that our trades are associated with and agree to work with them on election plans in their congressional districts. That way, each concerned industry can take responsibility for obtaining the best electoral results in specific states. You know what they say, 'All politics is local,' and it happens to be very true here.

"Telling our incumbents that local companies can help them stave off the primary challengers is probably the best leverage we have right now. While we can help raise campaign money for our local members, the muscle has to be applied where they live and work. Can we agree on this minimal agenda?"

A movie mogul spoke up, "I can't remember ever being so frustrated. Every road seems to come up against boulders, that cut off from both advance and retreat. We're trying to fast-fight the good guys without being bad guys. In my business that's a non-starter, at least from any saleable standpoint. Trying imagining Batman killing Superman and then pretending he was a nice guy.

"On the other hand, a popular revolt started by rats. Now that's a great plot and screenwriters are already at work on it, but they can't figure out how the story ends. So, it's stopped in project development hell. Not to complain about my own problems . . ."

A construction magnate trade representative was furious. "What! You are complaining about your problems. You are causing us problems. You are seriously telling us a movie is going to be made about the rats, with us as villains, no doubt. I'm torn up . . . But come to think of it, how can I blame you? This is how you make a buck, just business as usual for Hollywood. Maybe there's even a silver lining here. Could your writers give us some believable scenarios of how this all ends. And I don't mean one of those sappy-happy endings, that even my teenage daughter hates by now."

The hospital chain CEO tried to get his fellow whiners back to the point he had made earlier. "Now we're drifting, really drifting. Let's get back on track. Our fulcrum is the primary. If we can credibly convince our supporters in Congress that we can defeat their primary challengers, we'll at least get a respite, at least more months to stretch out in whereby we can have more time to put forth well-planned tactics.

"Such tactics cannot be developed on the fly. As I see it, we need to come out with some big exposé, an attention-getter that scares people into questioning what is about to happen. The Cooperators have cleverly shielded themselves from any 'isms.' Worse yet, they have lots of veterans in their midst, including some with Congressional Medals of Honor, and lots of social gospel religious leaders. Their wall is high, broad, and has few crevices that I can see. That's why we have to buy some time to figure out how to scale it."

"I have an idea," interjected the hoary trade association head for the giant chemical/pesticide corporations, "This might seem a little crazy, at least till you think it over. Why not return Congress to where it was when it had to be evacuated and could not function? Why not arrange for another massive invasion of rats?"

Some of the folks around the table were shaking their heads in disbelief, but he pressed on, "Why not arrange for the militant animal welfare groups—they're already furious over what they call 'the massacre of the rodent innocents' by the exterminators—to repopulate the offices and corridors, the cafeterias and the hearing rooms with those randomly behaving furry little creatures? This will cause Congressional operations to be suspended again and bring back the mockery, ridicule, and pillaring which launched this nightmare. By winding back the course of Father Time, we may see a wave of public distaste replacing the current wave of fevered reform. People will again get bored, not aroused, by Washington dramas."

The Hollywood mogul said to himself, "He should be one of my screenwriters."

And he turned to the Washington counsel and said, "Before you pass judgment on whether such a plan is sensible, can you talk about it from a legal perspective?"

The counsel said, "Clearly, anybody who floods the Congress with rats would be prosecuted, if caught, for criminal trespass and creating a public nuisance. Unless I am mistaken, these transgressions would be felonies."

The chemical/pesticide organization head was all business in terms of working out whether it could be put to the test. "If you are not mistaken," he said to the counsel, "that means we could always pay someone—say via a charitable contribution—to take the rap, serve out a short sentence, and live happily ever after. Is that correct?"

The counsel, though no enthusiast for this scheme, could divorce himself from his feelings and look at it from an objective legal standpoint. He spoke thoughtfully. "As the law now stands, you are correct. But if the solons get any wind of this, they'll turn this act into a first class felony in a New York legislative minute and charge you with criminal conspiracy."

A mega–media mogul was a bit flabbergasted by the absurd direction the discussion was taking. "What I'm hearing just doesn't pass the smell test. Even if you can figure out the logistics, fill the trucks, get past the guards without incurring mayhem and so on and so forth, it won't work. The prosecutors would consider this breaking and entering—a felonious act if there ever was one. Candidly, I think our brains have dried up from our unusual experience of powerlessness, so unless anyone has any better ideas, I say we stick with our esteemed hospital chain representative's suggestion, which boils down to: Every mogul for himself.

"I move to adjourn and return to the large conference room."

No one spoke, but everyone eyed each other a trifle suspiciously.

The media mogul reiterated the consensus, "OK, it's every trade group for itself. Devolution here we come! Importantly nitpicking the bills as suggested by clever counsel, here we come!"

"Second the motion," cried several trade magnates in unison.

"So moved. All in favor, say aye."

After hearing a chorus of ayes, the media mogul said, "The ayes have it overwhelmingly."

The Wall Streeters received the business reps conclusions with little surprise. The Chairman had said the two sides worked from slightly different rationales. He advised the lawyers in the room to return to their "exquisite skills of monkey wrenching," urged everyone to keep in touch, especially if they come up with new ideas, and, with a wink, declared it still the better part of valor to "keep writing those checks to our supporters on Capitol Hill." Whereupon, after some drinks and a nice repast, the weary Washingtonians returned to home base to be greeted by the Million Americans March, a rally that was coming together on the historic mall as the conference attenders landed at National Airport.

The Million Americans March

There never was a rally like this giant aggregation of an informed, motivated and widely representative populace who were staying for the duration, staying until the job was done. No weekend demonstrators here, leaving behind cups, cans, paper, and other debris as they exited town. All had post-rally assignments, including very respectful vigils in front of every house and condo harboring a member of Congress, including an ever larger ring around the Congress and the White House, their exploits carried out with the guidance of smart lawyers and logistic specialists and via Internet with very smart media relations colleagues.

The Reporter was everywhere, observing, interviewing, noticing the nuances of the assemblage's remarkable organization and division of labor. To give everyone additional ownership of this event thereafter, and to make sure the growing movement was funded as much by the grassroots as the sturdy oaks—the three billionaires—eighteen-inch buckets were being passed around for cash contributions, money that would be used to set up even more visible storefronts around the country and in the general Washington environs. There were thousands of empty storefronts in America ready to be rented cheaply and used as a clearing house/info shop/community activist center as a place to go about uniting neighborhoods and publicizing, in a hands-on manner, the grand drive for this supremacy of popular sovereignty. The organizers of the bucket brigades, backed by occasional exhortations from the large stage of speakers, estimated they had made a collection of some twenty million dollars, or an average of twenty dollars per person. Additional sums were pouring in from cell phone donations throughout the country.

The Reporter located and interviewed the people in charge of chanting the rolling rhythms that so enchanted the huge television and radio audiences, who were watching the rally. These chants had been crafted to display musical excellence, being led by expert chanters positioned throughout the crowd, thus keeping the tones at professionally consistent levels. The words of the chants were on point. One chant went like this: "Of, by, and for the people, the government will become; *not* should, *not* must, but *will* become or our society is really done." Another: "Justice, peace, and happiness will mark out time on Earth. To make this happen more and more, we must be good ancestors as never before."

Having interviewed people at the rally and soaked up the atmosphere, the Reporter raced back to his office to compose his words and analysis, beginning by playing off the words of one of the chants:

> Today was a day like never before. A million Americans who knew who they were, where they were going, and how they were going to get there, filled the Mall. In each of their hands was not a flag. In their hands was their agenda: the promise of America that would make our flag sing the words that climax our Pledge of Allegiance: "with liberty and justice for all."
> This was a grand audience, ready for a long haul, not drifting

away as happened so often to the sporadic uprisings in the decades before. The people at the rally have assignments they will return to after the day's excitement. These are tasks so specific that their reverberations are penetrating into the nation's Congress and White House. It's as if many years of frustration were being concentrated into days of demands, into a sense of self-discipline that throws in the toilet the myth that the common people can't take control of their own affairs, which has been promulgated through years of public manipulation and control of the many by the few. These are the few who pretend they are running things for everyone's benefit. But they are, in fact, doing so out of infinite greed and the lust for domination, passing on their techniques to daughters and sons so as to assure its perpetuation from one avaricious generation to another. And, folks, this is not me editorializing. I'm repeating the words I heard both from the grandstand and in the crowd at this mammoth rally.

"NO MORE," cried this assembly, whose members, judging from my spot checks, were possessed of an intelligence and sustained reflections on our nation's needs that were an antithesis to a mob's attention deficit disorder. Prepared and seasoned before they arrived and ready for interconnected assignments during their stay, this rally was no mere *tour de force*, nor a mere civic show of force. This was the serious vanguard, a million strong, fighting for that once distant ideal captured in President Lincoln's felicitous words—"a government of, by, and for the people"—rooted in the permanent presence of a new and renewable civic/political, American culture worthy of Lincoln's legendary words.

Working my way through the citizenry, I overheard what they were saying to one another in between the speeches, in which the speakers elaborated details of the twenty-four bills that were headed for enactment. In interpersonal talk that took place in this dense togetherness, the rally attendees discussed these bills and their own prospects in the future, a future of livelihoods that mattered, that were secure materially, where people cared for one another's work, leisure, family time, and for looking out for their descendants. The words of the people

Ralph Nader

in the crowd were not pompous and belabored; they were pictorial, describing a landscape where what Jefferson called "the pursuit of happiness," enabled by justice and confident freedoms. Everyone I overheard tended to end their sentences with a smiling, "No Big Deal, We Earned It."

All this may sound pie-in-the-sky, naïve, distanced from the raw realities. Whether it is a dream or an unconquerable movement, the next few months will tell. This time, these people believe, time is on *their* side.

Deeper Doings of the People's Revolt

Aside from the stick-to-itiveness of the members of this people's struggle, there was another major difference between this assemblage and those in American history that had preceded it. While effort had gone into setting up the rally, at the same time there was enormous parallel work underway in the city and in every congressional district. Doug Colebrook and the Cooperators were expanding their "arms together," one arm in Washington, the other in localities across the nation.

The original one hundred and ten AACs, now one hundred and forty-two, in Congress were spreading their influence day and night on Capitol Hill where the lights were burning way after midnight. Everything was substance, support, and timing. What went on in the AAC offices during those midnight hours was the checking and cross-checking of the post-hearing Committee report drafts, the encouraging of dissenting views, the working on the schedules for the oncoming House floor debates for each of the twenty-four bills, keeping the White House informed daily, providing the media with honest appraisals and details they demanded, not including head counts on different bills which AAC members believed crossed the line into punditry and pomposity when legislators pretended they had more votes than they probably had.

The Speaker, outraged over the impudence and coarseness of the counterattacks against the growing people's movement, increased his resolve to spread the views he expressed on *Meet the Press* among his House allies, in his words of counsel combining practical idealism with advice on ways for them to survive the primaries.

The Senate, as usual, was its own self, heavily reflecting its long-ingrained habits and its restricted procedures, which favored their being a super-majority consensus on a matter before it took any action. Somehow, all these characteristics seemed antiquated, downright musty before the rearing dynamism coming at the Congress from the people. The old Senate syndromes really didn't matter all that much by now. The super-majority was the American people; that was what mattered and the majority and minority Senators knew it.

The three billionaires and their "get it done" action men and women were flowing the money into all the right places. They were impressed by the bucket-brigade—not really needed, in their ample pecuniary opinion—but brilliantly devised to strengthen solidarity and give people a sense of self-reliance. Besides their money, these wealthy individuals—and were they ever "individuals" in the most libertarian sense of the word—found themselves now taking on the role of cheerleaders, buffing up the confidence of those who expressed anxiety over what could go wrong and scuttle this surge. The bona fide libertarian among them reminded the waverers that, in the past, Congress had acted with lightening rapidity given the pressures, as happened when President Bush turned the screws to instantaneously pass his version of the notorious Patriot Act in 2002. In truth, the billionaire added, pressure, relentless pressure, for speedy action sucks the oxygen out of the opposition whose key assets are delay and attrition.

Midnight oil, indeed. At a large, old vacated embassy, which Doug Colebrook and his radiating all-points Cooperators were leasing, it was literally 24/7. The meetings with their allies on the Hill were legislative-specific as the work went on with the expert drafters, the media explainers to the reporters, editorial writers, columnists and features writers. Within the social movement were endless stories, personalities, and collaborations with "unlikely allies" to be written about and disseminated. With only a few news reports of the sporadic grumbling by the trade groups and an occasional outburst by an enraged CEO, which garnered little audience share, the peoples' mobilization dominated the traditional media and, of course, the social media.

Counterrevolution on the Ropes

In record time, the Congressional hearings and their reports were largely completed. The votes to send the bills to the floor, and, in the House, on the discharge petition procedure to circumvent the still obdurate Rules Committee, were underway. There were unusually large numbers of abstentions by Committee members opposed to everything, but not willing to put this opinion on record so as to make them an easy target for their primary opponent. Their explanations for not voting, when asked, revolved around words like, "too precipitous" or "freighted with good intentions but bad unintended consequences."

Quickly composed were three kinds of opposition. First, many of the trade groups warned about "economic collapse," "a free-fall for the bond market," "mass layoffs," "an investment boycott," "a lowering of the government's credit rating," "corporate flight overseas," and other sundry, dismal predictions. When the press asked them to be specific, rather cuttingly, with such questions as: "How are improved public works; better housing; safer food; sustainable energy independence; fairer taxation; assistance to deprived children; overdue wage increases; cleaner air, water, and soil; law and order for corporate violations; and more honest elections with greater choices on the ballot going to lead to such calamities?" The questioned press offices were non-plussed. They didn't want to sound foolish, so they fudged, saying something about "the evils of bigger government" and, even more pusillanimously, said they would get back to the inquiring reporters, who themselves had to undergo some transformation and reinvention, for being a routine ditto head no longer cut it.

The second counterattack, if that word can be used, was undertaken by front groups paid to say and do what the corporate funders could not. It was too strong to describe the thugs they hired as "brown shirts," but these groups of young tough guys rallying, demonstrating, picketing, and taunting the massed activities of the people's revolt showed no restraint either in their words, placards, bullhorns, or threatening, but not fulfilled, demeanor. They tried to tar members of the social movement with words such as: "Communists," "Freeloaders," "Traitors to the American Way," and labeled the progressive movement as pushing for: "More Big Government," "More Regulation," and "Civil Rights for Rats," to mention only some of the more staid vituperatives found in their mouths and on their posters.

Were these front groups effective? Well, they did get on the media. But they were so extreme as to be a caricature, and even a fence sitter was more likely to label them as loonies than take them seriously. Moreover, when interviewed, they could provide few details behind their slogans. Worse for them were the probes by reporters that uncovered their being well paid, by the hour, by commercial interests opposed to the pending legislation. Still, the cameras couldn't resist showing them on the evening news for the sake of "balance."

The third approach was to marshal the business-funded think tanks, who were, by virtue of their regular work, able to be quick studies of what was going on so that they could handily churn out rebuttals of the AAC's bills and rationales. However, here the tanks and their commercial sponsors had to confront a problem: There were left/right concurrences of varying degrees on many of the proposals. While the corporate think tanks had learned how to run with their business grants, making sure their clients got their money's worth, they also tried to evince integrity by issuing occasional reports about "crony capitalism" and the wasteful spending on contractors, though these discussions were one-shot deals with little obvious follow-up.

A private meeting was arranged between the payers and the payees to iron out the dilemma or, as one staffer called it, "a sticky situation." The resolution they eventually came up with was quite forthright. The corporate foundations would provide grants to those who could present the strongest arguments against such and such proposed AAC reform or change. The grants would be openly announced in the interest of vigorous debate and discussion. Since the freedom train was already speeding on the tracks toward its destination, it was stipulated the work for which the grants were paying had to be finished in a very short duration, ten to fifteen workdays and done. The think tanks had most of the ideas, which would rationalize the status quo, already on tap and it would not take long for them to assign specific rebuttals to specific bills and their itemized provisions.

Of course, there were other pressure points besides the big three prongs of the counterattack where the reactionaries could bring influence to bear. To keep weak-kneed legislators in line, there were the specially placed campaign contributions, honorary dinners for supportive politicians, and post-Congressional employment hints. Also in the arsenal were the not-so-reliable leaks designed to hurt the AAC, such as supposedly "discovered" internal memos by giant multinationals, which "revealed" that if this or that part of the agenda passes, the firms would have no choice but to close down named plants and offices in named congressional districts and move their operations abroad where there is a "better business climate."

As far as swaying the minds of legislators, however, all these combined efforts only made a small dent on Capitol Hill in terms of changing minds or solidifying the backbones of waverers, for they were nowhere near as effective as the populations' *in personam* lobbying or the imminence of the primary challenges or the workings of the Speaker and his allies. As the leaders of the counter-reaction were learning, these corporate resistances worked best on persuading the persuaded, hardcore supporters in Congress and around the country. But that wasn't nearly enough to begin to change the momentum or shift the game from who was on the offense and who was holding down an anemic defense.

Of course, to go deeper into the underground that supported the status quo, there were always the privately-retained, shadowy private detectives looking for dirt, contemplating entrapments in compromising situations or nailing down bribes. But this type of skullduggery takes time to develop, involves the real possibility of boomeranging risks, and, besides, it is power that corrupts and the people's revolt was not yet in power so its members were relatively uninvolved in blackmail-friendly situations.

With one month to go before the first primaries, pervasive gloom and doom permeated the realms of corporate-dom. It is not as if their inner selves, which most had ignored for years, were so upset. These selves could see that if the reformers bills were enacted there would be a better country ahead, less risk of street chaos and a more prosperous middle class. But their outer selves—the positions and activism they were paid handsomely to maintain every day—were in full control of their possessors' personalities; and these shallow egos were wallowing in doubt, pessimism, and wit's end frustration. They weren't used to losing, and this contest promised to end for them in a gigantic beating. They weren't used to thinking creatively when they were stuck on the defense. So they hung their feeble hopes on the above-mentioned "counterattacks," knowing they were not even up to the Hail Mary, last-minute-save kind of scoring.

Ancillary Groups Push the Progressive Project Further

At about this time, four of the numerous ancillary street theater groups that had sprung up in the movement and whose performances had frequently gone viral on social media, displaying telling events and socially relevant artistries, asked for a meeting with the Cooperators and the AAC. Once inside a bug-proof room, they put an exciting proposal on the table.

Why not schedule a day for passage of each bill in both the House and Senate at which time the theater specialists would put together massive encircling demonstrations around the Capitol building? The demonstrators would take up peaceable chants like, "Pass Them, Oh Patriots" or "Vote for the Jeffersonian Revolution—No Big Deal" or "Give Us Your Better Angels, Congress."

"You know," one guerilla theater actress said, "we'd be using real positive language but an unmistakable, unspoken 'Or Else' as the subtext."

"It's the Skinnerian approach," added another organizer who was a Harvard grad and mime, "positive reinforcement."

One of AAC's brightest lights, Representative Ivan Incisor, who had quickly grasped the value and the possible weak points in the plan, said, "There are twenty-four major pieces of legislation scheduled. Are you sure you can sustain such intensity outside in all kinds of weather and with the danger of possible provocations that would invite a police crackdown?"

Zono, a world-famous musician who had become a leading promoter of events that raised money for progressive causes, replied, "To take your last point first, we are exceedingly aware of outside provocateurs who try to start fights or worse. That's one reason why we have worked to establish close and good relations with the police and why we have carefully placed our own arm-banded sentinels throughout the ralliers. We've even composed songs like "Ballad of the Lonesome Provocateurs." The reason for that is that we've discovered that the more we talk about troublemakers, the more expectant the public is that they will find them trying to infiltrate us and the less likely they will be to associate such disruptors with our side."

Zono readjusted his bandana and continued. "As far as being able to sustain the outside, dense presence daily, we have relays of backup brigades, as we call them. For sure, the same ralliers cannot keep the intensity up for twenty-four days. So we will put people in rotation. You may know, by the way, we have mobile medical and legal clinics, kiosks distributing free food donated by Busboys and Poets and other avant-garde restaurants as well as other kiosks that can help attendees with referrals to hostels or rooms available for modest rents for those who would otherwise be homeless or have to go back to their hometowns."

"You guys are more impressive than I thought," observed Senator Earl Morningside. He had been asked to attend this session although he was a fence sitter at this point. He was needed because he was such an expert on Congressional rules that he regularly impressed the scholarly Senate and House parliamentarians whose job it was to authoritatively interpret the rules. He gave them his take on the situation. "To begin, let me address the artists and others coordinating the outdoor actions. I understand, from my reading in history, how important an air of expectant success is for the progress of a social movement and that's something that your street presence conveys around the country. But, to turn to those working inside the Capitol,

I wonder how you are going to handle procedural points of order and privilege inside the Congress. I believe these will be thrown up like roadblocks and could stretch the time beyond the single day you have allotted for passage."

At this point, Doug Colebrook called on the AAC's own expert on Congressional procedure. The venerable scholar suggested that "the AAC may have the votes to change the procedures generically. The Constitution specifically declares that the Congress sets its own rules and, in my judgment, no more than a majority vote is needed to alter those rules."

"I guess you asked me here to get my opinion on that issue of Congressional rules, and I must say I concur," remarked Senator Morningside. "Though others may well challenge the majority vote point, it is my understanding that they will lose before the parliamentarians, who will agree with the professor."

On that point, the meetings with the ancillary groups were concluded and the deliberations resumed between the inside and outside forces around the table.

The first thing mentioned by a latecomer to the meeting was a news report just off the wires. He read it out, as it was brief.

> The public health experts and veterinarians retained by the House and Senate administrators to study the safety of allowing the continued admission of caged pet mice to the Congress have issued their report. So long as the pet mice are certified as healthy by a licensed animal lab, there is no basis to ban such mice brought as gifts to members of Congress or their staff or carried as pets.

Chalk up another victory for the rodents.

Sweet Home, Alabama

About the same time as the progressives were cheering the report of the victory for the mice, a quite different reaction was heard from another part of the country when the news was broadcast.

Deep in the heart of conservatism in rural Alabama, during a night when the air was filled with the musical renderings of a cacophony of crickets, a dozen males, who were seated in a dim saloon known for inviting outspoken views, heard the news about the pet white mice.

"What kind of horseshit is this?" exclaimed one drinker, Billy Phil.

"Liberal horseshit," replied another, Billy Frank.

Billy Joe chimed in, "These traitors are trying to cut down our military that protects our freedoms. That's what they're really up to." This was Billy Joe's favorite topic and it didn't take much to get him to talk about it. Now while the rats were not actually involved in fighting our boys, the mention of liberals had gotten him riled.

"You don't really believe that bullshit. Do you think a bunch of ragheads over there, fighting to get us and the Brits the hell out of their backyard so they can kick out their dictators, are losing sleep angry about our freedoms?" retorted a drinker wearing long hair and a surplus army jacket form the Iraq War. This fellow was not just imaging what a great soldier he would be if he had ever been in the military, as Billy Joe was, this new speaker, Billy Link, had been there, done that.

He continued provocatively. "You go in both directions, Billy J. First you tell us how much you hate the Feds here at home, and then you hoist the Red, White and Blue, backing anything the Feds do to brown people overseas. You're even willing to go to kill or die for the politicians and the Big Oil Companies that bankroll them. I mean you'd go if your lack of fingers, ones you lost in the mill, made it possible for you to enlist. C'mon, just because you're a redneck, like me, doesn't have to mean you're stupid."

"Billy Link, if I didn't know your mom and dad, I'd be tempted to deck you here and now. And don't think I couldn't do it, missing fingers and all. Did you forget we were attacked on 9/11?"

"Billy J, I'm not forgetting. I think I proved my patriotism in my military service. But, I'm asking you to contemplate how all this started in the Middle East back at the beginning."

Billy Joe scratched his head, "You mean cavemen throwing dinosaur bones at each other?"

"I don't think we have to go that far back," the veteran said. "Just go back to right after World War I. There were no states as we know them in the Middle East at that time. So, who carved up those territories, splitting machine-gunned tribes, making them separate states, and then who then backed their dictators, who have been killing and starving them from their palaces with F-15s?

"When I was overseas I read *War is a Racket*. You won't believe who wrote it: a double Congressional Medal of Honor Winner, Marine General Smedley Butler. He tells you how, early last century, he went to war for National City Bank in Cuba and the US oil companies in China. It's a short book with grisly pictures of dead soldiers lying on the ground. For who? For what? If you want to unlearn your ignorance, pick it up."

"Okay, okay, Billy Link, y'all cut it out," interjected Billy Phil. "I think you're mentioning reading is confusing Billy Joe. I don't think he does too much of that. No, just joking, man. What I'm saying is Billy Joe got us off the original topic of the rats in Congress. I mean the four-legged specimens.

"I know a rich guy. Don't worry he's a good old boy, like us, he just happened to make it big in real estate. He's got an idea of how to play a big ratty prank on the politicians. He wants to load up five eighteen-wheelers with tens of thousands of hungry rats and, in the middle of the night, unload them around and, if possible, inside the buildings of Congress throwing food around to keep them there. He'll pay his deliverers two hundred dollars an hour to get them up there. Any takers?"

"First, where's he getting all those rats?" asked fussy Billy Frank.

Billy Phil told him, "Brother, rats are not that hard to come by. My rich acquaintance knows someone who can just suck them out from the big cities underground, you know, from the pipes, the sewers, the tunnels. He said the whole operation could be done smoothly and fast. It's just largely a matter of moolah and he's got plenty. He wants to see what he calls 'the greatest show on earth,' on TV when the thousands of rats are unleashed on the whole damn crowd of pompous asses."

Ralph Nader

"Other than a long distance joy ride, what's this rich buddy of yours trying to make happen?" questioned Steve the bartender as he replenished some beers and wiped the counter. (He was a transplanted Northern so he didn't have the name Billy.)

"Beats me," Billy Phil confessed, "you know these loaded millionaires, they don't believe they have to explain anything to folks like us. He wants to hire us as truck drivers to just get the job done. I'll bet he has other motives—no doubt."

He threw in, as an afterthought, "But can't you guys use the green stuff? I sure can."

Beginning of the End for the Old Order

Back in Washington, the pace became ever more muscular and assured. The people were feeling their strength by the day. Reporters conceded as much in their daily filings, noticing in particular the swelling ranks of the "joiners," who were utilizing their capabilities to aid the movement in just about every task, with a panoply of skills and knowledge. Far from having to beg people to come to demonstrations, rallies, and planning sessions, the organizers had layers of reserves to enlarge the turnouts at events and to carry out the needed services at demonstrations, such as putting out the materials, helping with details and spelling those citizens, who had joined and committed their energies earlier, but at this point were tired and needed a break. That's what a galvanizing momentum does.

At a heavily attended news conference, the AAC and the committee chairs released the legislative schedule—one day for one bill—twenty four days in total with only Sundays off. Spring recess was cancelled. The first bill up was to be one that put forward a serious tax reform. The day chosen for its passage was symbolic, April 15th—taxpayer deadline day.

As the first B Day approached, there was a press-attended announcement of the full scheduling of the bills. At the event, an AAC spokeswoman talked up how carefully things had been prepared and orchestrated, praised the committee chairs and the diligent work of the committee members from both the majority and minority side.

She made sure the media was reminded of how thorough the committees and sub-committees were in their deliberations and mark-ups, and how receptive the majority was to having the minority file their dissents. She threw in that most of the twenty-four bills concerned subjects and recommendations which, if never passed before, had been publically discussed, debated, and reported on at length over the years and decades. No surprises, no trap doors, no legislative tricks.

When it came to their turn to speak, the committee chairs did not dispute anything she said. They limited their remarks to procedures and scheduling for the floor debates and named the floor managers for each bill.

And on April 15th, the remarkable historic process commenced. The joyous citizen assemblies, as expected, surrounded the Congressional buildings peaceably and at regular intervals changed, following their rotation plan.

Looking out the tall windows of the Congressional offices and corridors, the lawmakers, their staffs, lobbyists, the guards, janitors, and food servers could see nothing but orderly people with signs, balloons and broad banners, night and day, regardless of the weather. Cocking their ears they could hear, "Pass It, Pass It, No Big Deal, We Earned It."

Never had this happened before. In 1932, the bonus army of many thousands of World War I Vets walked, or traveled in other ways, to Congress, and set up camp. They were acting from despair over not receiving the money owed them for their soldiering in that miserable, bloody, avoidable war. They didn't have time to fully impact Congress as they were violently dispersed by the US Army commanded by Douglas MacArthur.

Nothing remotely like this dispersal was in the cards for this people's revolt. The Washington Police, the Park Service and the standby National Guard were on strict orders to avoid all provocations and maintain close communications with the organizers to head-off or minimize any trouble.

Inside the Congress, the corporate attorneys were preparing last ditch efforts to insert those amendments spoken about during the private meeting with the Wall Streeters. Neatly drafted and explained both technically and in plain English, they sought sponsors, working the rooms in search of bendable ears.

They were successful in finding a few lawmakers, who were willing to offer these amendments on the floor, doing so, embarrassingly, when everybody was looking. It took some real arm twisting to get a few sponsors. Not only were these legislators less than enthusiastic at being identified with a visibly losing cause, but they knew such amendments—dealing with lower budgets, weaker enforcement, and set expiration dates—were usually inserted during more secretive committee drafts via the offices of friendly staffers. In those cases there was no necessity of explaining the meaning of highly technical legalese. That flimflamming doesn't pass so easily during open floor debates. Still, the few suborned lawmakers went ahead with the requests because they were beholden and dependent on the customary political donations and tit-for-tat political friendships.

And so, day after day, with only a little slippage, the bills became the presumptive laws of the land, for the President had already signaled his desire to sign them in sequential White House people's celebrations. Had he not wanted to—and DooLittle being a very political animal understood this—it would not have mattered for the insurgents had the votes to easily override any vetoes.

The Quick Passage of Earth-Shaking Legislation Even Shocks the Movement

After the tax bill, came, in quick time, the food, housing, energy, health, and safety legislation. Each day's passage expanded the popular mobilization and excited expectations. Day by day, the naysayers, the negatives, the pessimists that one encounters in every community, shrank in numbers. Cynicism melted into skepticism, which soon melded into affirmative thinking. The hardcore ideologues who believe democracy is mob rule—the masses running amuck—remained rigid in their views, faithful inheritors of the thought of the early Tories at the founding of our Republic who called the people "rabble." One modern day Tory, in a West Texas restaurant, was heard to say, "Well, it's their time; let them have it. They're sure to screw things up and then it'll be our time once again."

After passage of the transportation, communication, insurance, and credit bills, a quizzical Doug Colebrook, lunching with his allies in the Senate dining room, asked his Senatorial collaborators how they could explain this unprecedented, phenomenal cave-in of the opposing members in both houses of Congress.

White-haired Senator Harrison Updike responded, "Doug, I heartily agree with your sentiment that what is going on is phenomenal, amazing beyond belief. Like you, I've been trying to understand what broke the dam and why all the dam keepers seemed to have abandoned their posts. Never seen anything remotely like this in my forty-four years here.

"I'd have to say it's a combination of factors that created a perfect storm—a storm on the lake which fronts the dam, as it were—against them and their interest group backers.

"First, above everything, is the timing. Everything in this agenda is long overdue and our opponents know it. How many stories have you read even in our usually compliant press of twisted corrupted budgets; unnecessary wars; Wall Street excesses; vastly overvalued CEOs, essentially paying themselves huge undeserved bonuses, fueled by useless stock buybacks, with the approval of a rubber-stamp-wielding board of directors; and greed draining other people's money? Haven't we read books, going back to Upton Sinclair and Lincoln Steffens, in which these crusading writers expose the domination of what people own by the monied interests, and describe how tens of millions are slaving away while financially losing ground?

"Tell you the honest truth, if this upheaval had happened twenty years ago, it wouldn't have been too soon. Not to pun, but at this moment, the congressional bills are almost the same as unpaid debtors' bills, ones marked long overdue. That means it feels like a perfect climate for an 'enough is enough' rebellion.

"Why didn't it happen twenty years back? That's the second factor, the human element. You, Doug, and the Cooperators put it together, quietly, insistently, and knowledgeably. You didn't do much vilifying, leaving it up to their primary opponents to wallow in the mud-slinging.

I can see why they scooped up the mud so fast. Those old farts weren't used to such challenges and they scared easily.

"Then there were the unstoppable marches, rallies, demonstrations that wouldn't go away and never stopped getting larger and more confident. If the fat cats and their legislative adjuncts were waiting for any petering out of the rallies and anti-establishment organizing, the type of gradual waning they had come to expect from past weekend demonstrations, they were sorely disappointed and shaken. Add the conversion of the Speaker and the knowledge that the White House was on the people's side—not surprising since its current occupant is a past master of repositioning himself the minute the wind shifts—and you could see the collapse coming.

"When the lobbyists read the tea leaves on the streets, and in the restrained quality of the legislative efforts and in the momentum on Capitol Hill, they couldn't present a united front and all their money couldn't guarantee wins in the primaries. Most of these corporate boys said to each other, 'Not enough time, we're not going to get in front of that train.' What's the phrase—*critical mass*—that's it. I guess in this instance a more appropriate term would be the critical *masses*, for once they joined their effort, with all the preparation so carefully done by you guys, they became what someone, I think it was the Reporter, labeled 'a vanguard of a million people.' At that point, what was considered impossible became a lot easier than anybody, anywhere, thought or dreamed. A vanguard of less than one percent of the people who support them back home. Whew!"

Other senators around the small dining table, with their mouths full, nodded in agreement.

Doug knew that when the lawmaking was over, the reporters were sure to descend on him with questions about the triumphs. That's why he particularly appreciated how Updike had mentioned all the people individually and collectively involved and needed for this victory. When the news people came calling, he wanted to respond so that the credit was not focused on him or even his core cooperators around the states. Journalists, even as they were leaving their ditto-head style behind, still had been trained to see everything being done in the world as the result of some great man or woman. Old press habits die hard. Doug wanted to fight against such pigeonholing of this story. It was his modesty, certainly, but it was more than that. He wanted the responsibility for making the whole effort work to be on the shoulders of all the people together.

He remembered jotting down in his journal, based on thinking about his readings of the history of the major revolutions and their destructive aftermaths of the past three hundred years, "The only revolution that counts is the revolution that works."

Another Week, Another Revolution in Lawmaking

The next weeks' menus contained such mouth-watering items as reforms in national security, public works, facilities for children, retirement/pensions, education, and civil rights/civil liberties. All sailed through Congress. These attracted even larger turnouts in the country's streets, squares, and ball fields. More women, minorities, and children were present. The following week more blue-collar workers, artists and entertainers, nature-lovers, and teenagers were in evidence in the inspired throngs that circled the Capitol and almost repopulated the city during the passage of the labor/work/wages, the leisure play/art, the crime prevention and enforcement, and the environment bills.

In the midst of all this exhilarating humanitarian/justice explosion, the storm sweeping away privilege and inequitable coercions, the staff was bedraggled, working literally sixteen hours a day. Some just slept on cots and couches in their offices, showering in the stalls previously reserved only for their bosses. But they had lots of bolstering from outside experts who had been marshaled by the Cooperators, from the mass-sports-level din of the rallies in DC and back home, who were applauding their actions, and from the inpouring of benign comments and praise from all sides, especially from the country's cultural, religious and ethical leaders, people so often ignored by the mass media.

Musicians and artists were no slouches as the avalanche of progressive bills were passed. They burst into the current news cycle when, for example, a country-western singer released a new ditty, one that shot straight to the top of the charts, with its signature lines, "Oh, what a beautiful country. Oh, what a beautiful Congress. Oh, what a beautiful country, everything's going people's way," sung to a tune taken from the famous Rodgers and Hammerstein musical. Lovers of *Oklahoma* were flabbergasted upon hearing "Congress" getting such an honor.

The final week of legislation was not without its perilous moments. It was in the face of the bills proposing clean elections with choice, the empowerment of the people, community self-reliance, and corporate accountability under Constitutional subordination that the entrenched corporate interests thought they had to make their last stand, drawing a last ditch line in the sand. They were smart enough to know that if these bills passed, there would take place heavyweight shifts in power that would make any future corporatist comeback difficult to achieve. The bills would remove the corporate domination of elections via their two-party toadies and would fortify the people's continuing stamina by providing many more full-time citizen advocacy institutions. They would undermine the global corporate power over local community economies and—the biggie of them all—strip the corporate entity of its personhood equivalence with real human beings, so as to subordinate the corporate system to the supremacy of our Constitution's increasingly atrophied but now reborn, "We the People."

A Line in the Sand at the Last Ditch

The Wall Street Chairman, who seemed dismayingly reasonable, wise, and accommodating to the demands of the progressive insurgency during his meetings with the Washingtonians, now protruded his fangs. It's been mentioned that he liked a good fight because that was the time when, his back to the wall, his aggressive instincts could get full play. Those who have seen him act in such circumstances, dubbed him, out of his hearing, "the werewolf."

If there was a method to his usual mildness, it was to bide his time and then, at just the right moment, launch out with the same sudden blitzkrieg approach that the insurgency was using: fast, furious, and targeted at the key nerve centers.

Before these last key laws came to a vote, ones that would break corporate power once and for all, the Chairman had arranged for a marathon session in Washington, DC. Much as he hated leaving his New York City prowling grounds, he jetted down for a weekend meet-up with nine super-fighters for corporate hegemony. He had calculated that between them they had a total of four hundred and sixty years of ferocious experience.

Not known for their overt fulminations, each having self-control that rivaled the werewolf's, eight of these persons were brilliant implementers of orders given by their businesses bosses. Their skills were testified to by the ample fortunes each had accrued. One was a masterful personal persuader in tone, logic, reason, and reassurance. Another was known as "carrot man," a guy who could make tough political decisions by the solons, ones that might undermine their standing with any voters paying attention, go down easier because of the goodies attached to the lawmakers doing the "right thing." A third was a smooth media man that no one had ever ruffled while he was getting his message across. (He was dubbed "the Buddha.") A fourth was known as "Mr. Stealth," the kind of person who negotiates in the dark recesses of the legislative process, with a makeshift office down to the Congressional print shops where he is something of an "invisible man," even to the printers working there. A fifth and a sixth were exquisite legislation-drafting experts who were intricacy nerds, unfazed by arcane cross-references to different statutes of multi-hundred-page bills. These are the masters of puzzle palaces for whom the most difficult chess games and crossword puzzles are "no problem." A seventh was a "Jim Farley" type (FDR's exuberant postmaster general), a glad-hander who knew every lawmaker, the staffers, the families, the children, and the birthdays, and made his rounds on Capitol Hill in order to prove it. An eighth was a CPA budget expert who worked for years in the White House office of Management and Budget, then did a stint at the Congressional Government Accountability Office (GAO), and then became the Chief of

Staff for the powerful Congressional Budget Office. He knew all there was to know about adding and subtracting monies from programs his paymasters favored or disfavored.

The ninth was a woman, an African-American lesbian, a well-paid token whose role was to help the Chairman discount any accusations of his ad hoc group being nothing but an extremely super-rich white men's club, which had no concern for the common people. Even bringing her on board had caused some grumbling among his associates. After all, when these males started, there were no women allowed to make the power climb; it was a time of several states even prohibiting women from serving on juries, a time when "Negros" could not even drink at certain water fountains, and cruel homophobia was publically unquestioned. The Chairman's *aide de camp*, who had found this triple-demonstration of diversity in one woman—a woman who was willing to follow orders as long as the price was right—received a large bonus. How absurdly out-of-touch they still were.

In her own right, this woman, a product of the poor education in people's rights offered at Harvard, believed that corporations should direct the nations' future because, unlike politicians, corporate types felt if they were not successful, they should be held accountable, just as business executives were answerable to their shareholders. And she was not only a token but displayed an awesome ability to argue this corporate "philosophy" when accompanying the others to selected Congressional offices.

Once assembled, the Chairman called on the hoariest of the attorneys among his "brain trust," who had seen and survived many a pressure cooker in his day, though perhaps never one quite like this.

"First off," the Chairman counseled, "I don't have to remind anyone how serious this crisis is, so let's think hard and act fast. Now, Jasper, please prioritize these four remaining mega-bills. Then, when you are done, we'll open up to everyone here for concurrence or critique and an action plan."

"Agreed, sir," replied the courtly lawyer with the penetrating eyes. Some, out of his hearing, said he had the eyes of a cobra. "It is my judgment, given the pressure of time and the political climate, that we can ignore the 'people empowerment legislation' with one exception. Let me quickly run down the reasons we can neglect it.

"It calls for a national referendum. We know how to deal with state referenda—look at California. We can live with that. It calls for easier access to the courts—which brings us back to the 1960s pre–tort reform—we can live with that. So will others," he added with a chuckle. "It calls for taxpayer 'standing to sue,' which, I believe, cannot be done by statute but only by Constitutional amendment, so the federal courts will throw it out.

"Now there is one part of the bill that is dangerous to the business community, and this is where I'm going to propose an exception to my policy of ignoring these irritants. It calls, most originally, for a variety of facilities or check-offs whereby companies will be obliged to carry invitations in their billings for consumers of different products they sell—for example, owners of motor vehicles or consumers of services such as banking, insurance, and utilities—to band together in non-profit advocacy groups. These associations would counter our superior power with their ample numbers of consumer lawyers, economists, scientists, accountants, public relations experts, and organizers. These groups would be voluntarily joined and mostly funded by the members and private grants, making them harder to attack. This facility idea represents a real power shift, but it would be very hard to assail since corporations have so many banding together facilities themselves. So our critics will be quick to ask, 'How can we object to such organizations when we have such facilities for our own purposes?'

"To internally sabotage this bill, I would say we should get our legislative worker bees to add one amendment: make these groups wildly democratic in the elections of their boards. That way they'll be likely to rip each other apart internally, as if they had an out-of-control defibrillator shocking their hearts. That's what's been happening with the board elections of the anti-capitalistic Pacifica radio stations, ruining their functioning. The more democratic the procedures, the more internally divided are leftist organizations and parties. We are drafting, shall we say, a 'counter-intuitive' pro-democracy amendment which is sure to get through. History is made by decisive leaders with authority, not by ultra democracy. That's why airline passengers don't get a vote in the air as to how to fly the plane.

"The other bill that doesn't seem to bring much trouble is the advancing of community self-reliance. First, it is non-ideological and invincible to amendments. Who can object, even indirectly through monkey-wrenching, to the general idea of self-reliance? It goes to our most fundamental values and origins as a nation. For god sake's, I know you aren't literary buffs here, but Emerson even penned a famous essay with that title. Also, who can be against farmers' markets or local solar power or producing locally more of what we consume or community health clinics or credit unions or community banks? I urge that we don't touch this one. I'm well aware in making this recommendation that our global corporate clients can see economic displacement on the horizon. Solar displaces the coal and oil companies, for example, or local food displaces the food giants or participatory sports replacing—well, not to be cynical—the expenditures for being out of shape and overweight, which include Weight Watchers, slimming drinks, and gym member-ships. But I say, let's not get too frightened over that prospect. Some of it we all want and is already happening. And please note there are eighty million members of credit unions whose net assets together don't equal that of one of the biggest Wall Street banks. Somehow, we biggies have managed to adjust and profit even with the increased presence of the little guys in business.

"That leaves two bills which are most serious threats to the way busi-ness operates today, or, to adopt the Occupy Wall Street people's phrase, to the 'one percent' and its purported privileges and pleasures.

"One is the bill that would give us clean elections with choice leg-islation that could seriously undermine business's influence over government. I don't have to remind you that the government we have worked so hard to mold to our interests is in many ways an accounts receivable department for us, an immense honeypot of contracts, lease-holds, grants, tax escapes, and a dazzling array of subsidies that keeps many corporate law firms buzzing with lucrative retainers. Take away government-as-usual and its welfare state, and we'd see consumer demand shrink and our business deals, from the military to public con-struction to extractions of minerals, far less robust. So let's look closely at the key provisions of this bill.

"First is exclusive public financing of campaigns. This has to be a Constitutional amendment in order to override several US Supreme Court decisions concluding that money is speech. Our opponents know the Constitution is involved and are using this chance to start the Constitutional amendment process. Like us, they realize this is only the start of a long haul to get three-quarters of the states to ratify. So, we have plenty of time down the road to block this one, even given the current tumult of the masses. We all know about powerful State Speakers of the House and Presidents of the Senate who rule with iron hands and have proven themselves in our cause repeatedly.

"The second provision relates to federalizing ballot access for federal elective offices, taking the power away from a mélange of state laws, most of which are real hurdles for competitive third parties or independent candidates. If this were put into effect, there would be tons of viable candidates who were not sponsored by our two understanding parties. This would cause us headaches, giving voters a place to go and increasing the pressure on the two parties to adopt measures not for our benefit. In short, a competitive electoral system is not to our advantage. Right now, we are quite happy with the two parties we have, ones that are constantly on their cell phones with us, dialing for our dollars.

"The third provision establishes voting as a legal duty with a fifty-dollar fine if a citizen doesn't vote and has no medical or other valid excuse. If this imposition were passed, it would make all the clever ways that have been devised to confuse or obstruct people of certain classes and races from voting both an obstruction of justice and a crime. So, voter turnout will rise sharply, as it did in Australia when similar laws were adopted, to over the ninety-percent level from the present thirty percent to sixty percent in Congressional and Presidential elections respectively. Those tens of millions of Americans who will be forced into voting are largely not our supporters.

"The fourth provision establishes a binding none-of-the-above (NOTA) line on every ballot to give voters a chance to say 'no' to all the candidates, a vote of no confidence. If NOTA wins the most votes, that election line is cancelled and a new election with new candidates will be scheduled in sixty days. Voters would love NOTA, but candidates don't like this one bit. Imagine how humiliating if NOTA beats them. This one I'm unclear on. With mandatory voting anyway, it is hard to see how it really disadvantages us. I don't really know.

"The last major provision ends gerrymandering by the states. Electoral districts will be demarcated by nonpartisan commissions, as in Iowa and a few other states. There is a constitutional issue here for the federal government requiring this, but it is muted with the proposed grant incentives to the states. However, I don't think this is enough to clear the constitutional question for objecting states.

"My take is that this law is so toxic we have to oppose it in its entirety. The argument we can go with is that it's an example of government coercion when people are penalized for not voting. The NOTA provision weakens this argument but we do not have to mention that in our campaign. Coercion is coercion. Just hit that note hard and often in our propaganda.

"Now for the last legislation, which is the biggest prize for these lunatics: dehumanizing the corporation by stripping it of its personhood and, therefore, its constitutional rights. That is what our opponents mean by 'Constitutional subordination.' We lose this fight and, mark my words, the next thing you'll see is legislation prohibiting corporations as corporations from lobbying, testifying, and making campaign contributions. Our effective use of the civil rights and civil liberties laws and the equal protection clause of the Constitution would be eliminated. You would see state laws banning corporate ownership of lands—as if, perish the thought, only individuals could own land. You would see laws requiring all radio and television broadcast licenses to be held by individuals, not by corporations of any kind. The entire set of shields that immunize corporations or allow them to act with impunity will be jettisoned. I'm just giving a few examples of the domino effect. So, here I say we have to go all out to defeat it because if we do not succeed, it is all over for the corporate world as we have known it. This is the bill that would spell the doom of everything for which we stand. The inclusive statutory wording even includes limited partnerships under the bans. These fanatics hold nothing sacred.

"Finally, as with the other legislation, these last bills have been expertly drafted by very skilled counselors. I am forced to say that they are breathtaking in their tight defense against advantageous ambiguity, waivers, exceptions, procrastination and such. However, what they cannot control is the year-in and year-out budgeting decisions. Once this hullabaloo is over, that is where we can inflict some useful starvation with our friends on Capitol Hill. So, even if they pass everything, all is not lost. I've said my piece; thank you for your patience."

The Chairman, with obvious delight, said, "Thank you, Jasper. That was a virtuoso performance. You have shown us exactly where and how battle must be joined." The Chairman turned to the whole table with his next remark, "So, let's get down to strategies. And I'm expecting intensive, no holds barred exchanges among all of you. Act as if your life was on the line, for maybe it is."

Whereupon, for over three hours, the Chairman got what he asked for as the other eight plunged into the details, the tactics, and the strategies. What emerged was a general agreement with Jasper's putting the focus against the two bills. There were a few minor disagreements. The Jim Farley type cringed when he heard the phrase they were going to use in their communiqués, "dehumanizing the corporation," which might strike some of their adherents as a trifle absurd. He was seconded by the smooth media-man, and they won a replacement phrase, "degrading the corporation." The "carrot man" advised that by openly conceding all the other bills, thus testifying to their willingness to compromise, they added credibility to their cause as they took on the ones so close to the bone. Everyone agreed that the "going too far" lament was a good psychological approach.

The Chairman was pleased with how the worthiness of each person displayed itself seamlessly in the intense discussion. He had never put these allies together in one room and hadn't been sure if things would click so well. The only exception was the "sleuth," whose talents were drained by the openness of everything. He was ready to make any effort to help the team prevail, but no one had called upon him—yet!

Once on board in agreeing on what to oppose, the talk bore down on the nature of the campaign. They boiled down their approach to a conventional, all-points counterattack that would touch all the bases: mass media, personal contact, well-placed campaign contributions, and unleashing small businesses back home. One key part of the plan would be setting up local news conferences of "ordinary citizens" which would exhibit "minute-men" images of just plain folks challenging big government's compulsory voting demand. These common folk, presumably,

Ralph Nader

would prepare huge petitions saying: "Hell, no, we don't have to vote." These would be brandished in parades with ostentatious veterans wearing their old military uniforms marching smartly in front. Having given the "people's revolt" activities full play, the media, they believed, would have to report on any corporate backlash.

The Cooperators' millions were not taken by surprise by the strenuous attack fielded against these last bastions of the economic royalists. The people's champions had advance warning and prepared all their demonstrators with bumper stickers, buttons, posters, and banners emphasizing the importance of these two bills, which were based on the undergirding principle: the absolute necessity of the supremacy of popular sovereignty over corporate entities. They encouraged debates at the community level to arouse a populace almost daffy with the previous successes.

Much of this clash of "who rules" occurred during about ten days of recess that the corporate lobbyists succeeded in obtaining in order to give the campaign breathing space. Congressional leaders were so exhausted by then that it did not take any arm-twisting to get them to announce the recess. What a ten days! The broadcast and cable media, the social media, the blogs, were all lit up with what more and more Americans were persuaded was a titanic struggle between real people and artificial entities that don't bleed, don't die for their country, don't love or have children or revere their ancestors. Poets, novelists, and musicians all found different ways of conveying the difference between a human and a business entity, emphasizing again and again how absurd it was for an advanced society to be run by what law professors called "legal fictions," corporations that could create their own parents called "holding companies," create their own decoys called, "shell companies," in tax havens. And many of them made sewers themselves out of our world's waterways, air, and land, where they could dispose of their toxic defecations.

Over and over again, artists and activists lambasted the double standards privileging corporations, soulless beings with lurid, coercive technologies which were ever more absentee, ever more removed from any sense of patriotism or loyalty to community, ever more demanding of government guarantees. The movements' diatribes, satires, and reasoned arguments sank deeply into the souls of the masses who were massing to rip off this cross of iron that hung around their necks.

Nuke 'Em

On the third day of the recess, the Chairman and his tight circle of nine decided it was time for the "nuclear option." They were going to plunge the economy into a downward spiral in order to scare the country into second thoughts on degrading the corporations' powerful status.

One advantage of concentrated plutocracy for the royalists, was that when a group wanted to get something done, they didn't have to reach many of the plutocrats to get the desired action underway. After tightly encrypted messages and personal meetings over one day, the bond and stock markets started to shudder and crash. Within forty-eight hours, trillions of dollars of pension fund and mutual fund paper assets were shrinking. Credit started drying up. Banks moved to increase their foreclosure actions. The dollar began a free fall. Contracts and construction projects were put on hold. Workers started getting pink slips or were furloughed. It was a terrifying display of leverage by a tiny number of power brokers, giving veracity to long-time corporate critics, so long ridiculed.

The downward drift of the economy hit Congress like a lightning bolt. Members knew it was planned, so obvious was the carrying out of this last ditch attempt. It was even easily discernible to the oligarchs' leading cheerleader—*The Stall Street Journal*—whose editorials couldn't hide but could justify such deliberate scheming as necessary to "save the republic and the free enterprise system." That known and said, the legislators looked apprehensively to the response by the multitudes behind the Cooperators.

Speculation was rampant. Would the people panic and run for cover for fear of losing what little they had? Would they say, OK, we got plenty with the other bills that have passed Congress, so let the fat cats have those two before these big boys flee the country with their riches and bring the whole economy down on our heads. Unfortunately for the

Ralph Nader

self-styled "masters of the universe," the vanguard in Washington, DC, and their stalwart allies back home didn't budge. In fact, they called out the Wall Streeters as "unpatriotic saboteurs of the American dream," "twenty-first century traitor Tories," "speculators selling America short in the stock market," and "bluffers who will blink first because they've got the most to lose."

The last pejorative was prophetically chosen as it did become a game of bluff played out over seven frightening days. The Wall Streeters knew they were playing with a fire that if it got out of control, could consume them. They were gambling that they would get what they want and then everything would rebound in the economy and the stock markets would re-ascend to where they were a couple of weeks ago. And the Chairman and his crew were not wrong in thinking this tactic would put heavy pressure on the Cooperators and their followers, who began to worry that as workers lost their jobs and savers started losing their money, enough of the popular rumble would begin turning against them that the momentum would be broken, taking the pressure off the opportunistic politicians in Congress.

On day four of the Chairman's "D-Day" counterattack, the negotiators on both sides met in the elaborate offices of the House leadership. Like two giant bulls with entangled horns, they pushed and shoved. The AAC emphasized that the two priorities that were scaring the hell out of the Wall Streeters—total public financing of electoral campaigns and the end of corporate personhood under constitutional subordination—were proposed constitutional amendments, rather than enacted legislation.

AAC stalwart Senator Horace Mills tried to calm the cornered Wall Streeters, "Remember, these two proposals still have to be ratified by three-quarters of the states. Our bills are just starting the process of possible Constitutional amendment. You'll have plenty of time and opportunity to argue your case state by state.

"That's the sweetener. But our group also has a contingency plan, which you may interpret as a threat if you wish. If you do not back up, we have a plan to nationalize the banks, start ten new banks—each with thirty-billion dollars in capital, giving them over three hundred and fifty billion dollars each in loan capacity—and to require the Federal Reserve and the Treasury to use the fuller authority we will provide them to reverse the downward spiral of the economy, which appears to be the final twist of your extortion game.

"I think those measures should allow you to understand that we have in our circle experienced people of your ilk. They know the games you play in 'disaster capitalism,' and how to defuse them. Remember, government created you through state charters, and we can re-create you in the way we like through overriding federal charters. Your call."

Jasper Arrington, the hoary lawyer, also known as snake eyes, took the field for the Wall Street team. "Clearly you all believe you are holding all the cards, given the tightness of time before the primaries. Your surmise is probably correct for the short run. But beware of pushing us too hard and gaining a Pyrrhic victory. You will have won the first round but bear in mind what has happened to societies that deeply alienate and dispossess their business community, losing its irreplaceable skills and operational know-how, which are essential in making the economy run smoothly.

"I know you folks say we can learn from looking back at the lessons of history so let me draw something out of the past. About seventy years ago, a prominent judge, Learned Hand, gave an address on liberty. He said, among other things, that liberty contains the sense that you may not be right all the time.

"In this spirit, I have been authorized to put on the table, our proposal that in case your two constitutional amendments turn out to be truly harmful to our country, you would agree to an expiration date after which the country can decide whether to renew, refine, or let the amendments expire in the light of their past experience. Should you add a six-year sunset provision for both, we'll call off the dogs and go back to our business. We can't vouch for all the business lobbies concurring, but our forces represent most of the immediately deployable influence. We will, should you agree, hold a joint news conference to eliminate any ambiguity or any normal public doubt."

AAC Coordinator, Representative Ray Bray, looking around the room at his colleagues, absorbed enough silent language vibes to see they needed to discuss this so he asked for a three-hour recess.

Ralph Nader

Weighing the Wall Streeters' Proposal

Once inside a secured room, everyone started talking at the same time until their chair, Senator Elizabeth Dimasio, quieted them down. But before they could get down to business, there was a shocking interrupton. Everyone's cell phones were ringing off the hook, to speak metaphorically. It was with news that three suicide bombers had attacked the US embassy in Asfurastan, killing thirty-five Americans and native staff.

"One of our worst nightmares," exclaimed Senator Russell Swift. He was always quick to see the implications of unfolding events. "Here comes, along with the necessary responses, a lot of distraction and demagogy.

"However, we can face that situation later. We have to come to a quick decision on the Wall Streeters' new *quid pro quo*. I say, give them the expiration date clause. It will expire after the next presidential election, which they hope will bring a hardliner into office. I firmly believe in the people's strength, magnified in the new playing field created by these new laws we have already passed. When it comes time to renew the Constitutional Amendments, the people will be solidly behind it. I'm not concerned about them. What is worrying is the Wall Street crowd and their adjuncts. I sense an awakening, sleeping giant, caught unawares by our precipitous assault on the system, which is now beginning to find its legs and its language of fear. We partly can stall this development by a timely compromise.

"Moreover, with a sunset provision, we're more likely to get the states to ratify, in that they realize this Constitutional Amendment is temporary, subject to reversal if it proves problematic. Also, our passing the final bills will not have to overcome misleading ads and publicity with the Big Boys calling off the dogs here. Though I have no expectation that their baying packs won't resume at the state level, trying to hinder state passage of the amendments. That's what happened with the ERA."

He ended by calling for further input, beginning with, "So, what say the Cooperators?"

The group saw the wisdom of his words, and after some further debate and analysis, went back to the Wall Street gang with a statement. It was not that they agreed with the insertion of the sunset clause, but that they were willing to bring the proposal to their adherents and see how they reacted. If they were favorably disposed, then the Wall Streeters would get their clause.

Harmony had reigned among the assembled Cooperator representatives but the next twenty-four hours were something again. First the proposal was floated over the mass media with the affirmation and explanations of the Cooperators and the AAC. It was going to be put to a vote.

"It is now up to you working on the state legislatures," the two groups averred in a joint statement. "If you don't like this six-year sunset provision, you can defeat it. It is fitting that the last judgment will be in your hands, state by state. You have been deliberating in small study groups on the importance of public campaign financing and Constitutional subordination of corporations to your rule. Our independent poll will commence immediately, as undoubtedly will those of the commercial pollsters. We urge a *yes* response. *Yes* will call the bluff of the Wall Streeters who think their deal will split our consensus and, given the economic turmoil, break up our phalanx into warring sides. We all—you and us—need to decide quickly. We await your wisdom."

The polls came back between 2 to 1, and 3 to 1 in favor of the compromise, with ten percent undecided or having no opinion.

A People's Celebration of a Job Well Done

The bills were passed one day after another amidst a record outpouring of public demand, joy, and demonstrations. Even the inclusion of the sunset clause, which was an unexpected setback, hardly damped the enthusiasm of the celebrants. One million people massed on the Mall to roar their support for what the large majority of Congress was passing on those especially historic last days. *In personam*, fact-based and righteous lobbying had proven itself *unstoppable*, working all the way from inside Congress to the US's farthest reaches in Hawaii and Alaska. With so much left/right convergence back home, the losers in the Senate and House took it quite well due in no small part to relief over their sense that their willingness to compromise and the extraordinary amount of work accomplished in the last few weeks would improve their prospects in the upcoming primaries. For Congress could not be called out for inaction, gridlock, or being in thrall to the corporations anymore.

The President joined in the praise of the senators and representatives, their staffs, and all the citizens who organized and pressed their national legislature into such long overdue enactments. He promised the "largest collective bill signing ceremony at the White House and its sprawling lawn in American history—right on Memorial Day." He added that day was fitting, in as much as, with the passage of these game-changing bills, "the elected representatives paid full tribute to the memories of our founders and the promise they held forth for these United States."

With unsurprising dispatch, the stock markets started to recover and the economic projects, investments, and credit, so many of which were put on hold, were back in gear.

Re-Girding Their Loins

The weary Wall Streeters and the Washingtonian lobbyists went on their vacations to rest and recover before initiating long-range strategic planning for the new era and the battles at the state level over the proposed Constitutional amendments that, let it be said, had received well over the required two-thirds vote in the Senate and the House of Representatives.

As for the *Stall Street Journal*, its lead editorial was titled, "Lo, the poor American people," and what followed was a list of premonitions featuring one forthcoming disaster after another and ending with the sentence, "Closing down the Republic and bringing on the chaos and instability of extremist democracy is no cause of celebration by any cerebral citizens."

With almost all the media attention on the winners, the Reporter, a contrarian as ever, wrote article after article on the losers. His commentary, along with his report, gauged the bitterness, backlash, and second-strike capabilities of those who might want to roll back the legislation in whole or in part. To his surprise, he found an eerie acceptance of their losses among the business class and its government associates. After all, the Reporter reflected, the people's victory did occur fair and square, without dirty tricks, or any autocratic blockage of their dissenting voices or the customary vituperatives that winners often hurled at the losers before their victory. The Reporter ended his observations with the question, "Can the overwhelming sense that the people collectively have spoken be ushering in a new moral tone and a new kind of belonging by Washington's politicians?"

Doug Colebrook and his colleagues were bone tired even as they knew their work was just the end of the beginning. Implementation was the challenge in the coming months as, if things went as they imagined they would, citizen turn-outs dwindle, people inevitably drifted away, and the normal rhythms of social life resumed. Fortunately, the new laws foresaw that for the democratic turn to take hold there was the necessity of many new civic groups starting to engage. Their formation was facilitated under the People Empowerment Law. Although knowing they would have to come back soon enough, the modest Cooperators returned to their homes and to many deserved public recognitions.

Rats Romp Again

During the ten-day recess, right after the bills were passed but well before the White House signing ceremonies, five eighteen-wheelers left their respective southeastern cities at midnight. They had previously rendezvoused in cities along the way, starting in New Orleans, to pick up their cargo: tens of thousands of rats, male and female. After two days, parked, as prearranged, at out-of-the-way, farm driveways, and three nights of travel, they arrived at their destination—the Congressional complex of buildings. Having trained and rehearsed rigorously, the drivers, being the four Billies (Hal, Link, Phil, Rank) and Steve, took up their positions, confident in their success and unafraid if they were busted along the way. After all, they had each been advanced several thousand dollars on their pay, been provided with free, experienced attorneys in case they needed them, and had souped-up getaway cars, ready for action and quick escape to be used after they stranded the trucks at different points of entry to the Congress and its massive office buildings.

These trucks were no ordinary vehicles; they were equipped with advanced telecommunications, radar, and catapults, ones that would operate silently to safely hurl the rats right next to the buildings in record time. Other long vehicles, loaded with fine bits of rat-delicious snacks and little globules of water, would use mechanical apparati to spray the areas near the buildings, entrances, sewers, and other apertures with meals to guide and entice the rodents into heading toward the Congressional underworlds. Another truck sprayed cat urine on the outside perimeter streets to discourage any rodents roaming away from the building complexes.

All of this amazingly was accomplished between 3:00 pm and 3:30 am. The bare bones Capitol Police, relaxing after nightmarish weeks of overtime, were, shall we say, inattentive if not downright nodding off or snoozing. In case any of them became alert and started rushing toward the trucks, naked women and men were standing in convenient shadows, ready to walk out and be arrested for indecent exposure as totally shameless faux prostitutes, who would serve as useful decoys for the few minutes required to distribute the rats and their bait.

The videotaped infrared operation came off smoothly. As soon as they hit ground, the rats were clambering over everything: stairs, chutes, gratings, and garbage containers, munching happily on the provided food. As the truckers and their assistants were getting into their cars and speeding away, the police started to appear. Their first actions were to accost the naked decoys, searchlights came on, sirens sounded. Meanwhile, the rats were momentarily granted free passage, the noise and disturbance extra incentives for them to jump down the nearest grating or other opening. By the time, the cops paid attention to them, it was too late.

The venomous, big, pissed-off rich guy who was watching from hundreds of miles away on his satellite TV, couldn't have been more pleased. Until, that is, in the morning, when he learned that an entirely different interpretation was being given by the media to the spectacle of returning rats, which he had taken care to videotape for further use. It wasn't long before he turned away with disgust over how his plans, so carefully implemented, had boomeranged.

It so happened that the Reporter, sound asleep at 4:30 am, heard his phone ringing insistently. Picking it up, he heard a low, mature voice tipping him off to what just occurred: "Rats everywhere around the Capitol. Friend, if you want a scoop, better get over here."

From long experience, the Reporter could usually tell whether calls like these were from cranks or reliable tips. This call sounded legit. Fortunately his apartment was three blocks from the Rayburn House Office Building. He leaped out of bed and was at the wild rat invasion scene in fifteen minutes. It was a wild scene. Police cars, fire trucks, ambulances, flood lights, blocked roads, and the first responders, all of whom, in the Reporter's view, were trying not to smile, laugh, or joke at the absurdity of it all.

He learned that other police cars were trying vainly to chase down the getaway cars, which seemed to have been driven by Indy 500 racers. Other cops were snooping for clues in the abandoned rented eighteen-wheelers. He also saw that the assembled crews were not making any effort to catch or kill the swarming, darting, disappearing rats. They were taking their stations, a couple kicking at the rodents, and waiting for the convoy of exterminators to show why they were so named. Since no lives nor property were at risk, and since they knew it was not part of their job description to go rat hunting, there was almost a festive air. The last few weeks had been pressured, what with the people's revolt and the nightmarish security demands they entailed. The Reporter sensed all this and approached some of the police and firefighters with questions:

"How's this compare to the first rat invasion earlier this year?"

The officer he'd approached, a burly fellow with a cruller in hand, was glad to answer him, "Well, it's a mystery how they got here. The earlier rats seemed homegrown, having been born underneath the buildings.

These fellows seem to be immigrants. Could be someone with a nutty sense of humor have dropped them off here?"

A firefighter hooking a small ax to his belt joined the conversation. "I wouldn't be surprised if someone's been spending a lot of money to get this far just to land a big joke. People will do anything for a laugh these days."

Another officer strolled over and spoke. "The way I see it, it's not aimed at the legislators. No one is in the Congress 'cause it is an official recess, so everyone went home for some R&R. That means whoever cooked up this crazy rat invasion didn't have any political objective. Or, if he did, he never consulted the Congressional calendar. Pretty bad timing I'd say. The train has left the station."

A sergeant joined the group around the Reporter. He did begin with a literary reference, "As a reader of novels, my guess is that this is someone's idea of irony. A lot of novels end with the hero or the situation having come full circle. The originator of this new rat incursion could be thinking he was closing the book on this wild spring the way it opened in the winter: rats out, rats in."

Eureka, the Reporter got his opening line, took the sergeant's name so he could credit him, and, after taking some pictures of mice and men, rushed back to his apartment to start writing.

I've just returned from Capitol Hill where, around three o'clock in the morning, a massive rat celebration took hold of the grounds. The rodents must have come from the grassroots of America: tens of thousands of them had been jammed in five eighteen-wheelers and then, arriving in our city, were catapulted to the earth and cement in and around all the buildings. Other trucks used high pressure hoses to spread all kinds of food rats love in the same area, which got them to openings that led inside the buildings and their underground rat alleys. Needing no other prompting, the rats dived right in to their new home.

All the trucks, after offloading, were abandoned by their drivers who took off in other cars and have not been located.

Obviously, the staging of this entire rodent theater piece

took lots of preparation, lots of successful secrecy, and gobs of money. For what?

Well, after interviewing some of the police and fire-fighters on the scene, I've come to share their opinions that it's someone's idea of a celebration of rats to commemorate what their earlier cousins accomplished in jolting the Congress to stand up for the people. That someone wanted you, the people, to recognize that both "we the rats" and "we the people" did this all by ourselves.

Of course, I can't prove my interpretation is correct, and the rats aren't talking. But what's just as remarkable are the streams of people who have been heading down to the Capitol grounds since dawn. They are coming, it seems, from every direction: Maryland, Virginia, even the District of Columbia, which is not known for joining in national events organized by outsiders. From what I saw, they are coming in ever increasing numbers, people from all backgrounds and all ages wanting to join in the celebration of the rats who are finally getting their overdue recognition. It looks like the public plans on being there for a while. The food carts and trucks are setting up shop in anticipation of a whole day of a dancing, singing, and speaking to each other festival.

"Stay tuned, your Reporter is racing back to the Capitol for more close contact, more eyewitness accounts . . .

Party Time II

The fast-forming grand scene stumped all the reporters similarly arriving at the first branch of government and its spacious surroundings. None of them could identify what was behind it. Literally thousands of women, men, and children were coming by the half hour. Who planned this turnout? Who had the credibility to make so many people believe that they had to be part of this historic celebration of the return of the rats? A half dozen reporters huddled together to exchange speculations.

"Some super-rich guys probably set up this shindig," said a guy from the *Daily Barnacle.*

"The same ones who delivered the rats after midnight," said another, the crack reporter from the *Washington Toast.*

"That's not credible," said the more skeptical fellow from the *Lie Busters Journal.* "We know it is very hard to get people out into the streets under any conditions and timetables. And this eruption of so many diverse, unconnected folks had no planning time at all."

"You old timers have to get hip to the new social media," said an online journalist from *Media Hype.* "My guess is that a bunch of social media bloggers, who have been on this whole story for months, had an instant sense of what good theater and copy this would be. So they collaborated on announcing a full day of wild celebration. You know how fast these guys think and form meet-ups."

Whatever the ruminations of the media, the massing throngs were sprawling all over the grass and cement with uninhibited, happy spontaneity. They hardly cared who prompted the event. They were dancing with rats, between rats, and over rats. The rats themselves, zeroing in on the newly appearing food and water—had they entered paradise?—at first scurried this way and that way, avoiding the people while snatching at fallen food on the run. But it wasn't long before they realized that these were different kinds of humans than those they were used to. These folks were friendly and had no intention of chasing and hunting them down. Rats are fast learners and pick up cues very quickly. So, like pigeons, they flitted in between the people snatching food and drink here and there, and from the human viewpoint, seemingly having a great time. The photographers and video guys were having a field day catching some of the most amazing juxtapositions in modern visual history of humans and rodents.

Predictably, spontaneous speakers on soapboxes began popping up. A duet belted out something they called the "Rat Serenade," complete with guitar and drum. A more somber lady was carrying a basket of $2 bills, which she handed out while exclaiming: "Are you glad they showed up on July 4, 1776, to sign the *Declaration of Independence* from

their cruel rulers? Now it's our turn to show up to control our rulers."
(The $2 bill has Thomas Jefferson on one side and a picture of the
founders on the other.)

Hundreds of dancing revelers plucked the $2 bill and held it aloft
as they pranced in all directions. Others wore masks to allow less
inhibitions, as did European medieval persons from all classes during
the annual Feast of Fools. Possibly, some legislators or money men
were concealed behind these disguises, people who didn't dare reveal
to their colleagues that they were rather pleased at the people's (and
rats') victories.

Even some of the police dove in, dancing away and when faced with
passing, slightly shocked glances, shouted, "Hey this is what community policing looks like!"

As the day wore on, soapbox orators focused more on the overall
invasion of the rats. Animal rights advocates were quick to take advantage of a once-in-a-lifetime opportunity—the attention of a huge
audience who were primed to recognize the amazing value of a hitherto
despised species. Both past and present were evoked in the encomiums.
One orator listed the legislative achievements of the rats, which were
about to be signed into law by the President. While another provided
an anthropological perspective, namely, that long ago on Easter Island
in the Pacific, the natives considered rats a delicacy as well as a luxury,
which evolved into rats becoming a means of mediation or barter
between different clans. The speaker cited Canadian master media analyst Marshall McLuhan as the source of this information. Many people
were fascinated, but the vegetarians drifted away the moment they
heard the culinary part of the narrative.

All this activity was streamed or went viral and so the crowd swelled
and spilled over from the immediate grounds and streets to the larger
park-like areas next to the Senate Office Buildings, then onto the large
Mall. Helicopters hovering about estimated the numbers heading
toward two million, noting that they would present a huge security
problem if they go out of control.

Not much chance of that. Too many troubadours, poets, artists were
doing their thing everywhere. As the day entered the afternoon, Doug
Colebrook and his Cooperators came back to DC and spread out into

the mass. They soon learned that the people who were part of this great turnout often had been contributors to the events inside and outside of Congress following the rat invasions and the awakening of America turning around the Congress and raising the great public expectation that "Now Is the Time to Get it Done" as one college student blurted out.

Meanwhile, the rat density was thinning out even as human density arched upward. Fed and watered, the rats had reached satiety and were looking for quiet dark corners and subterranean sanctuaries where they could engage in either sleep or normal intercourse with each other. As the rats diminished their numbers, some among the multitudes began heeding the appeal of several "soapbox" speakers, only, in this case, the "soapbox" was on the back of pickup trucks, equipped with loud speakers. They were calling on people to sign regally designed petitions. The lines to do so grew longer and longer. These scenes went viral and the electronic signatures from millions of watching citizens around the country poured into the collectors' computers.

Tribute From a Grateful Nation

What were they demanding? That a GIANT BRONZE STATUE OF A RAT IN DEFIANT, FEROCIOUS POSE BE ERECTED ON THE CAPITOL GROUNDS TO BE MAINTAINED IN TIPTOP CONDITION IN PERPETUITY. THE INSCRIPTION ON THE BASE OF THE SCULPTURE IS TO READ: "IN GRATEFUL MEMORY OF THE INTREPID RATS THAT FOLLOWED ONE ANOTHER INTO THE PRIVATE PLACES OF OUR LAWMAKERS AND LAUNCHED THE AMERICAN REVOLUTION OF 2018!"

And so it was duly built and dedicated on Thanksgiving of that year by the President and Congressional leaders before large admiring crowds of grateful Americans already starting to have their livelihoods and quality of life and its prospects benefiting.

It was nearly midnight on that Thanksgiving eve, after the public had scattered when a shadowy figure approached the statue and gave it a long silent salute. It was Speaker Blamer. And as he walked off, he could be heard whistling "The Times They Are a-Changin'."

THE END